KV-058-447

CRh

DATE DUE			

girls will be girls

girls will be girls

 THE NATIONAL TRUST

introduction

'What is bettre than wisdom? Womman.
And what is bettre than a good womman? Nothing.'

Geoffrey Chaucer, *Tale of Melibee* (*c.* 1390)

'Language', said Samuel Johnson, 'is the dress of thought', but seldom is it appreciated how feminine her attire can be. Many of the words and expressions with which we decorate our speech are intrinsically feminine in origin, and often we are not even aware of it.

The full experience of woman can be found buried beneath metaphors, similes and everyday expressions – and a rich and full experience it is.

Mythology gives us goddesses and heroines. Names such as Aphrodite, Juno, Calliope, Penelope and Pandora have filtered intact through time, and one of the mightiest rivers in the world is named after a legendary female warrior. The ancient world provides clever and powerful queens, and the echoes of women such as Helen of Troy, Dido of Carthage, and Cleopatra of Egypt are still amazingly resonant. Faith inspires courage and conviction and saints like St Catherine, who is commemorated in a spectacular fire-work, while Mary Magdalene is the source of 'maudlin'. Folklore abounds with fairies and magic that help expressions such as 'pumpkin time' make perfect sense. And art and history make up the deficit.

The talents, toils, hopes, sorrows, fears, loves, curiosities, dreams and delights of womankind can all be found in common words and phrases – many of which have been fashioned by men. Authors from Chaucer to Shakespeare and Dickens to Coward, have created heroines whose names pop up in familiar phrases. You may not know, for example, what an 'Alice in Wonderland Scheme' is *exactly* but you, no doubt, will know the story to which it alludes. And you are sure to have a 'Mrs Malaprop', or an 'Aunt Edna' somewhere in the vicinity.

Then, there is fame and fashion. From corsets we get expressions like 'strait-laced'; 'petticoat government' is an anathema to most men, and what about that scanty swimsuit named after a tiny Pacific atoll, or the life jacket named after a Hollywood legend?

Girls will be Girls is an exploration of all of these and much more.

Some of the expressions are flattering, some are not. Some are serious, some amusing. But all provide a glimpse into the fascinating world of women and illustrate how the fairer sex have contributed their fair share to the glories of the English language.

Abigail

A seventeenth-century term for a lady's maid, the name Abigail has biblical origins. In the first book of Samuel, Abigail saves her husband's household by providing food for David and his followers and beseeching him to listen to what she, 'thine handmaid', has to say. A waiting gentlewoman in the play *The Scornful Lady*, written by John Fletcher and Francis Beaumont in around 1613, was called Abigail, perhaps in deference to the biblical character, and following the success of the play the name became a byword for a lady's maid. It is thought that the term gained wider popularity during the reign of Queen Anne (1702–1714), one of whose ladies-in-waiting, Abigail Hill, was a particular royal favourite.

African Sisters

A popular name for the nymphs in Greek mythology who, with the assistance of a dragon, guarded the fabled garden on the Isles of the Blest where golden apples grew. As daughters of Hesperus, the Evening Star, they were known collectively as 'The Hesperides' and their home was considered to be the western extremity of the earth.

After Us, The Flood

The English translation of 'Après nous le déluge', this phrase is attributed to Madame de Pompadour, the extravagant mistress of King Louis XV of France. She is reputed to have come out with the term in response to being taken to task for her lavish excesses and wastefulness. The implication is that nothing matters once you are dead, but the expression has also been cited as a premonition of the French Revolution.

Agony Aunt

The term, first recorded in the 1930s but not gaining wide usage until forty years later, is used to describe a woman who offers help and advice on personal problems and anxieties, usually via a column in a newspaper or magazine. It is thought that the term is an extension of the Agony Column, the popular name given to the personal column in newspapers of the late nineteenth century where people could publish messages to missing relatives and friends and where the 'agony' of human existence was consequently displayed. Curiously, it was in the magazine *Fun*, published in 1863, that the term Agony Column was first mentioned in print.

Ale Wife

The term for the landlady of a tavern, it is also the name of a fish belonging to the herring family, so called because of its stout appearance. While the words beer and ale are now almost interchangeable, originally ale was a malt brew without hops. In medieval times, ale was brewed predominantly by women using fermented malt which they made by steeping grain (usually barley) in water, allowing it to germinate and then drying it slowly in a kiln. Although hops were grown in Britain after the Norman Conquest it was not until the sixteenth century that the Dutch idea of using use them as an additive to ale to produce beer was recognised.

Alexandra Rose Day

In 1912, as part of the celebrations to mark her fiftieth year of residence in England, the Danish wife of Edward VII established one of the first 'flag days' to be held in Britain. Thousands of ladies, many from the aristocracy, were recruited to sell wild roses in London to raise money for the hospitals and charities that Queen Alexandra supported. On 26 June 1912 the sale of the roses raised £32,000 and it was decided to make Alexandra Rose Day an annual event.

Alice Band

The illustrator, Sir John Tenniel, originally drew Lewis Carroll's eponymous heroine with long, free-flowing blonde hair in the 1865 *Alice's Adventures in Wonderland*.

Six years later, in *Through the Looking Glass*, Alice is drawn with her hair held back off her forehead by a wide headband. The popularity of the style and the book ensured that such bands became widely known as Alice Bands and are still referred to as such today.

Alice Blue

In the 1970s a slang name for the police, because, it has been suggested, of the colour of their uniform, the term Alice Blue stems from a gown worn by President Theodore Roosevelt's daughter. The particular dress, a light greenish blue, was the subject of a song written for Alice Roosevelt when she was sixteen by Joseph McCarthy and Harry Tierney. In Britain during the 1930s another song 'The Girl in the Alice Blue Gown' was popular.

Alice In Wonderland Schemes

The children's book, *Alice's Adventures in Wonderland*, was written in 1865 by an Oxford mathematician, C. L. Dodgson, using the pen name, Lewis Carroll. The book was a great success and with its sequel, *Through the Looking Glass*, it is considered to be a classic. In both books, Alice finds herself in bizarre and unaccountable circumstances and consequently any scheme which was implausible, impractical or just plain silly became known as an Alice in Wonderland scheme.

All My Eye And Betty Martin

There are various ideas as to how this expression, a synonym for 'stuff and nonsense' came into being. The one most commonly quoted is that it is a British sailor's translation of an Italian plea that he heard abroad, 'O, mihi, Beate Martine', meaning 'Oh, grant me, blessed St Martin'. (St Martin is a very popular saint being the patron of many different strata of society including soldiers, reformed alcoholics, beggars and winemakers.) Another idea is that there was a real Betty Martin in the eighteenth century – an acclaimed actress – who was rather fond of the dismissive expression, 'My eye'. It is agreed, however, that the expression can be found in a letter written in 1781 by a certain S. Crispe which begins: 'Physic, to old crazy Frames like ours, is all my eye and Betty Martin . . . '

Alma Mater

The term, used to describe someone's former school or college, is Latin for 'mother who nourishes'. Originally the Romans used the expression to refer to several goddesses noted for their bounteous natures. In seventeenth-century England the term took on the meaning we know today, reflecting the idea that educational establishments were considered to be centres of intellectual and spiritual nourishment.

Amazon

A strong, large and aggressively capable woman is sometimes referred to as an Amazon, in reference to an ancient tribe of Greek legend. According to the stories, the Amazons were a race of fierce women warriors who burned off their right breasts to allow them to use their bows with greater ease. Amazons were said to tolerate men only as domestic servants, for procreation or as suitable opponents in battle. The Maranon River, the world's second longest river after the Nile, was renamed the Amazon, by the sixteenth-century explorer, Francisco de Orellana, after he claimed to have seen imposing, frightening women on its banks. In ancient Greek, amazon means 'without breast'.

Amy Darden's Horse

During the early nineteenth century in America, Amy Darden's horse became a symbol of dogged determination. During the American War of Independence, a troop of soldiers had requisitioned one of the Virginian widow's horses, but had never returned nor replaced it. When all Mrs Darden's efforts to seek recompense failed, she took to petitioning Congress — and did so for nineteen years. Finally in 1815, thirty years after her horse was taken, she received the compensation she had been seeking. The expression 'Amy Darden's horse' became a byword for persistence in the face of legal obstinacy and delay.

Amaryllis

Familiar as a houseplant which bears spectacular blooms, Amaryllis was originally the name of a country girl in the pastoral poems of Theocritus, Virgil and Ovid and came to be a term used to describe any rustic belle.

Angel Water

This was the familiar name of a scent popular with women in the eighteenth century. It originated in Spain and was made of a mixture of roses, myrtle, ambergris and orange-flower water. The perfume took its name because originally it was made predominantly of angelica, the 'angelic plant'.

Annie Oakley

The theatrical slang term for a free ticket is so called because such a ticket used to be punched with a hole to ensure it could not be returned to the box office for resale. The reference is to one of the most famous trick-shot experts of all time, Annie Oakley. Her real name was Phoebe-Ann Moses, one of eight children of an Ohio farmer. Even as a young girl she was recognised as a remarkable shot and she eventually went on to become a star of Buffalo Bill's Wild West Show, which toured America and Europe to great acclaim. One of her tricks involved tossing a playing card into the air and shooting out its centre before it hit the ground. The resemblance of a free ticket to one of Annie Oakley's bullet-perforated cards led to the expression becoming common parlance.

Answer To A Maiden's Prayer

A term used initially to describe a handsome young man or an eligible bachelor, it is now also used to describe anything that perfectly matches what is needed at any one time.

Aphrodite's Girdle

Any woman who is irresistibly attractive to the opposite sex is said to wear Aphrodite's girdle. The allusion is to Aphrodite, the Greek goddess of love and beauty who was judged to be the most beautiful of the goddesses. According to mythology, Aphrodite wore a belt that caused anyone who saw her to fall in love with her.

Apron String Tenure

For centuries the laws concerning a woman's property and her husband's rights to it were clear cut – what was hers became his when they married. The situation was often more complicated when it came to a husband's rights to the property of his wife's family. In some cases a husband was entitled to enjoy the use of such property while his wife was alive but could not claim it as his own. Such an arrangement was known as 'apron string tenure' and it could be ended if the couple divorced. It was generally considered that a man in such a position held the weaker hand and in time the expression was used to describe any seemingly indulgent submission to a woman.

A Stitch In Time Saves Nine

The wisdom of this proverb is self-evident: making minor repairs promptly prevents the need to undertake larger, more time-consuming repairs later on. It was a proverb known in Roman times when the poet Ovid used a variation in his verse.

Aunt Edna

In the world of theatre an Aunt Edna is someone who prefers conventional plays about conventional subjects and who espouses conventional morality. The term was the creation of the playwright Terence Rattigan. He described Aunt Edna in his *Collected Plays Volume II* (1953) as: 'A nice, respectable, middle-class, middle-aged maiden lady, with time on her hands and the money to help her pass it . . . Now Aunt Edna does not appreciate Kafka . . . She is, in short, a hopeless lowbrow . . . Aunt Edna is universal . . . she is also immortal.' In America, an Aunt Edna is known as 'the little old lady from Dubuque' and can claim a longer pedigree. She came into being via Harold Ross, who was editor of *New Yorker* magazine in the 1930s. Ross suggested that 'the little old lady from Dubuque' needed to be taken into account when deciding moral considerations in relation not just to the theatre but to all topics of life.

Aunt Sally

When someone becomes a scapegoat, especially when unfairly so, or a subject of ridicule, he or she can be said to be an 'Aunt Sally'. The allusion is to the centrepiece of a popular nineteenth-century fair or carnival game. It was a figure of a woman's head with a pipe in her mouth at which players would throw sticks with the intent of breaking the pipe. While it was common, and had been for centuries, to refer to any old woman as Aunt – the original Aunt Sally is thought to have been a black-faced doll based on a character in *Life in London* created by Pierce Egan in 1821. Apart from becoming a fairground game, the doll's face also served as a shop-sign to indicate second-hand clothes were on sale.

Bachelor's Wife

The perfect or ideal woman was known as a Bachelor's Wife – the implication being that such a woman does not exist. The expression comes from a proverb: 'Bachelors' wives and old maids' children be well taught'.

Bad Hair Day

Everyone knows that a woman's hair is her crowning glory and that on the days when she 'can't do a thing with it' life can take on a gloomy aspect. In the 1990s the term became a concise way of explaining the feeling of life being out of control or out of kilter. American, and specifically Californian, in origin, 'Bad Hair Day' can also be a metaphor for being in a bad mood.

Baker's Wife

This sobriquet was given to Marie Antoinette, Queen of France from 1774 to 1793 and wife of Louis XVI. The king's unsuccessful efforts to appease his people's furore over the cost and shortage of bread led to him being nick-named 'The Baker', and consequently the extravagant and dominating Marie Antoinette was dubbed 'The Baker's Wife'.

Barbarella

The heroine of a French comic strip in the magazine *V* made her debut in 1962. She was heralded as the new breed of woman – sexy, blonde and smart enough to be an astronaut – albeit one who had a tendency to fall out of her clothes. Jane Fonda brought Barbarella to international attention when she starred in the film of the same name in 1967.

Belles Of St Trinian's

The schoolgirls created by the artist, Ronald Searle, originally as a series of cartoons, still live on as the epitome of everything demure young ladies should *not* be. Searle produced his cartoons from 1941 to 1953 and they appeared in magazines such as *Lilliput* and *Punch*. Then in 1954 the first of the St Trinian's films was made, the *Belles of St Trinian's*, and the school and its pupils won a firm place in the affections of the nation. St Trinian's girls were more interested in drinking, smoking, gambling and getting their own way than they were in any form of academic study and their comic exploits delighted millions. *The Wildcats of St Trinian's*, the last of the five St Trinian's films, was made in 1980.

Beauty Is In The Eye Of The Beholder

This is an accepted truism that encapsulates the idea that what is appealing to one person may not be so to another. An early version of the proverb, which appears in John Ray's *English Proverbs*, published in 1670 is: 'An ass is beautiful to an ass, and a pig to a pig.' Later, the philosopher David Hume, put the sentiment more eloquently in his 1742 *Essays Moral and Political*: 'Beauty in things exists merely in the mind which contemplates them'.

Beauty Is Only Skin Deep

This well known proverb has been recorded since the early seventeenth century and suggests that one's strength of character is of greater importance than outward appearance. The writer, H. H. Munro (better known as Saki) added a rider to the saying in a story from 1904, *Reginald's Choir Treat*, when one of his characters asserts that, 'Beauty is only skin deep, but ugly goes right to the bone'. It is thought the writer was using a shortened version of an old Leicestershire proverb, 'Beauty is but skin deep, ugly lies the bone; Beauty dies and fades away, but ugly holds its own'. The French equivalent of the expression is 'Beauty without virtue is a flower without perfume'.

Beauty Sleep

Any sleep these days is considered to be valuable but originally the sleep thought to be most beneficial to one's appearance was that taken before midnight. George III was adamant in his belief that seven hours of sleep a night were appropriate for a woman. Men, he thought, could survive on only six.

Bee In One's Bonnet

This expression used to describe the idea that someone is obsessed with a particular notion or subject was first recorded in the mid-nineteenth century in the works of Thomas de Quincy. In the sixteenth century the term used instead was 'bees in the brain' and it was female fashion that wrought the change. Bonnets, hats without a brim at the back and usually tied with ribbons under the chin, became popular in the early nineteenth century and for more than eighty years were worn by married women as a sign of their status. In his book, *Crowther's Encyclopaedia of Phrases and Origins,* 1945, the writer Edwin Radford dismisses the expression as 'an exceedingly bad metaphor. There is nothing aimless or stupid about the buzzing of bees'. Nonetheless, the expression remains extremely popular and well used.

Behind Every Good Man Stands A Woman

Almost proverbial in the truth it espouses there are endless variations on this expression. The idea that success needs support was originally seen as being that offered by a wife. However, several wits over the years have added their own spin on the saying. Groucho Marx, for instance, is reported to have said 'behind every successful screenwriter stands a woman. And behind her stands his wife'; and the American politician Hubert Humphrey in 1964 claimed that 'Behind every successful man stands an amazed mother-in-law'. A more recent, anonymous, variation is 'Behind every successful woman, stands a man asking "where are my socks?"'

Belle Of The Ball

An expression used to describe the woman or girl considered to be the loveliest at any particular gathering. 'Belle' is the French for 'beautiful' and balls were once important social occasions, particularly as part of the 'London season' when eligible young ladies were introduced into society. One of the most famous balls is the Queen Charlotte's, first held in 1925 to raise money for the maternity hospital of the same name and held annually at the Grosvenor House Hotel until 1976. Part of the ceremony involved the debutantes of the year processing past and curtseying to a huge cake made specially for the occasion. The Queen Charlotte's ball was revived in 1989.

Best Bib And Tucker

When going to attend a special occasion, you are often advised to wear your 'best bib and tucker', although the actual items mentioned went out of fashion long ago. A bib was the top part of an apron, and a tucker was a lace or muslin frill which women in the seventeenth and eighteenth centuries wore over their dresses to cover their necks and shoulders. In time the expression widened out to include any finery of the day, regardless of the actual items of clothing and today your 'best bib and tucker' are simply your best clothes.

Better Half

Originally this was a term to describe a person's spiritual persona, the idea being that man consisted of body and soul and that the spiritual half was superior. It was Sir Philip Sidney, in the sixteenth century, who first applied the expression to marriage in *Arcadia*, which he wrote in 1580. Although it was used to describe either partner, it became more common for a man to allude to his wife as his 'better half', in deference to what, some might say, is an honest appraisal of the situation.

Bevy Of Beauty

Although there are various explanations available as to the origin of the word 'bevy', the *Oxford English Dictionary* says its origin is unknown but that it is considered to be Middle English – that is, dating from somewhere between about 1150–1450. It is the collective noun for quails, larks and also a company of maidens or ladies. The alliterative appeal of a 'bevy of beauty' is undeniable.

Biddy

Used in America as a slang term for an Irish maid-servant, Biddy has also long been an abbreviated form of the girl's name Bridget and used as a colloquial term for a chicken (an abbreviation of the dialect word, 'chick-abiddy'). In eighteenth-century England a 'biddy' was a young woman – but in the succeeding hundred years the term became mostly associated with older women and prefixed as such. An 'old biddy' is a term for any older woman, especially one perceived to be a bit of a busybody. In Australia, however, 'biddy' remains a slang term for a female teacher.

Big Bertha

The nickname for a 420-millimetre heavy howitzer manufactured and used by the Germans during the First World War comes from Bertha Krupp, who inherited her father's enormous steel and armaments empire after he committed suicide. Although her husband, who changed his name to hers, became the titular head of Krupp industries, there was never any doubt as to who wielded the power and Bertha was known by the workers as 'Queen Bertha'. The cannon, which unofficially took her name, was a massive affair and needed a crew of hundreds of men to move, clean and prepare it for firing. Initially the gun could fire shells over a range of seven miles, but successive modifications improved its range to a remarkable seventy-six miles. It was used to devastating effect in 1918 in the shelling of Paris.

Big Girl's Blouse

It is thought that this late twentieth-century term, used to describe a man who is rather wet and something of a sissy, comes from the North of England. It is sometimes associated with the television actress and comedienne, Hylda Baker, who starred in the television series *Nearest and Dearest,* but its exact origin is unknown and its reference obscure.

Bikini

The scanty two-piece swimsuit designed by a French motor engineer, Louis Réard, was originally called *le minimum* and was the smallest possible item of clothing that could still legally be considered as such. In the wake of the US atomic bomb tests on the tiny Pacific atoll of Bikini in the Marshall Islands in July 1946, Louis Réard renamed his creation *le bikini.* Some say it was because the effect of the swimsuit was as explosive as the tests had been and others that the reference was simply to the minute size of the Bikini Atoll. Whatever the truth, the bikini has been a fashion staple ever since.

Bimbo

While being the Italian word for baby or little child, when it popped up in English in the 1920s 'bimbo' was used as a disdainful term to describe an attractive but dim person of either sex. It was not until later that it came to be a dismissive term specifically applied to young women. In the 1940s

P.G. Wodehouse, however, was still using the term in its broader sense when he wrote about 'bimbos who went about the place making passes at innocent girls after discarding their wives'. The word came into vogue again in the 1980s and scores of 'bimbos' appeared in the tabloid press, usually on a 'kiss and tell' mission. Teenage bimbos became 'bimbettes' and male bimbos 'himbos' or 'bimboys'. In the 1990s the word 'bimbo' marched on. Nowadays 'power bimbos' or 'killer bimbos' are terms used to describe women who have the traditional qualities of a bimbo but who also enjoy successful careers.

Black Maria

The van used to convey prisoners is said to take its name from a formidable black woman called Maria Lee, who ran a boarding house in Boston in the early part of the nineteenth century. Enormously strong and prodigiously large, Maria was held to stand for no nonsense from her sailor boarders and gained a reputation for being ready to help the police take prisoners to the cells in her own van. When the British police force introduced patrol wagons in the 1830s it is claimed that they were nicknamed 'Black Marias' in her honour.

Blonde Bombshell

The original Blonde Bombshell was the actress Jean Harlow who starred in the film of the same name in 1933. (Actually in America the film was called simply *Bombshell* and it is thought the word 'Blonde' was added in Britain so as to make it clear it was not a war film). The expression is now used to describe any attractive fair-headed woman with an imposing personality, particularly actresses and celebrities.

Bloody Mary

This excellent vodka and tomato juice cocktail, a staple of Sunday brunch, was devised by a barman called Fernand 'Pete' Petiot, at Harry's Bar in Paris in the 1920s. There are various suggestions as to how the drink got its name but the most celebrated is that it's named after Mary Tudor, Henry VIII's devoutly Catholic daughter by Catherine of Aragon. When Mary came to the throne in 1553 she was determined to restore papal supremacy to England. During her five-year reign she put nearly 300 Protestants to death, an act which earned her the sobriquet, 'Bloody Mary'. As for the drink, it has become one of the world's most celebrated cocktails and there is even a book, written solely on the subject, by Christopher O'Hara called *The Bloody Mary: A Connoisseur's Guide to the World's Most Complex Cocktail*. There are numerous recipes but according to Georgiana Cecil writing in *Country Life*, 'The only rule governing this most versatile of cocktails is the time at which it is drunk: never before 12 and always before lunch.' A Bloody Mary made without vodka is known as a 'Virgin Mary' or, in some circles, a 'Bloody Shame'.

Bloomers

A New York social reformer and women's rights activist, Amelia Jenks Bloomer, is responsible for the term. In the early 1850s Mrs Bloomer adopted the fashion of wearing a close-fitting jacket and a skirt which reached to just below the knee, under which were worn 'pantalettes' or Turkish trousers that gathered at the ankles. Although not her own invention, the outfit rapidly became known as the 'Bloomer Costume' because of her high social profile. In England the trousers were deemed to be especially suitable for young ladies interested in pursuing sporting activities such as bicycling. In time the term 'bloomers' was used to describe the loose, knee-length knickerbockers that became fashionable and eventually became synonymous for any knickers at all.

Bluegown

There are hundreds of expressions in English to denote 'a lady of the night' or harlot and 'bluegown' is just one of them. It comes from the fact that from the late sixteenth century onwards the uniform for prostitutes held in a House of Correction was a blue dress.

Blue-Eyed Maid

This rather gentle term was used by Homer for the goddess of Wisdom, Crafts, Arts and Rational Warfare, Minerva – the Roman equivalent of the Greek goddess, Athena. There are various symbols associated with

Minerva and her diverse interests, including helmet and breastplate, an olive tree and an owl.

Blue Rinse Brigade

A slightly pejorative term to describe middle-class, elderly woman thought to hold outdated views. The allusion is to the washing of grey hair with a blue rinse to enliven the colour – a hairdressing trend which was introduced after World War II and which became very fashionable in the 1950s. By the 1960s the expression as we know it today was already accepted and instantly conjured up the image of women set in their ways. An article in *The Times* on 15 March 1999 used the term to good effect when it was headlined, 'Drive to make JPs blue collar, not blue rinse'.

Blue-Stocking

An erudite woman with intellectual interests has been dubbed a 'blue-stocking' since the term became fashionable in the late eighteenth century – and it has not always been complimentary. Historically, upper class women were meant to divert themselves with non-intellectual pursuits but, following a trend in Paris, various literary circles gradually appeared in England during the 1750s. A Mrs Elizabeth Montague established such a group in Bath and one of her most prominent members, a Mr Benjamin Stillingfleet, always wore blue stockings – an idea the rest of the members soon copied. Such a precedent had been set in Venice in 1400 when an intellectual circle was established called *Della Calza,* the badge of membership of which involved wearing blue stockings. There was a time during the nineteenth century when the term 'blue-stocking' was used to imply that any woman interested in academic or intellectual pursuits must be lacking in femininity. The idea gained so much common ground that the French philosopher Jean-Jacques Rousseau is quoted as saying, ' A blue-stocking is a woman who will remain single as long as there are sensible men on earth.'

Bodice Ripper

The term belongs firmly to the latter part of the twentieth century, even if the subject to which it originally related does not. In the publishing world a 'bodice ripper' was a romantic novel, usually historical, which involved the seduction of the heroine. The reference is to the fact that the plot of such books often included the ripping of the bodice of the heroine's dress by the impassioned and impatient hero. Since the 1990s the term has been extended to describe any romantic novel, especially those with a racy plot. The historical element may no longer be necessary in 'bodice rippers' but the seduction element remains inherent to the genre.

Bottle Blonde

A slightly bitchy term used to describe a woman who is not a natural blonde. In the beginning of the twentieth century the more common expression was 'Peroxide Blonde', alluding to the use of the compound hydrogen peroxide as a bleaching agent for hair.

Bottom Drawer

When a woman starts collecting items in preparation for married life, she is said to put them in her 'bottom drawer'. Traditionally the bottom drawer of a chest of drawers was the largest and where a girl would store the linens she had made for the occasion. In Anglo-Saxon times it was considered essential for a young woman to spin from her own thread a complete set of table and bed linen before she was deemed suitable for marriage.

Boudoir

The word comes directly from the French *bouder*, to sulk, and a boudoir was the room in the house to which a woman could retire when she wanted to be alone or to entertain intimate friends. It derives from the name of such rooms that were set aside in the Palace of Versailles for the various mistresses of Louis XV, during his reign from 1715 to 1774. In eighteenth-century England a lady's sitting room commonly came to be called her boudoir rather than being another separate room.

Bra Burner

A woman who shows solidarity with the feminist movement is often dismissed as a 'bra burner'. The term stems from the 1970s when women liberationists were encouraged to burn their bras, and many did so, as a physical and symbolic gesture of setting themselves free from the 'tyranny' of male oppression and sexual fantasy. It is claimed that the first bra, or brassiere, was invented by an American, Mary Phelps Jacob, using two handkerchiefs and a ribbon. It is said she sold the patent for her invention in 1914 for the sum of $15,000.

Bride-Laces

During the sixteenth and seventeenth centuries it was common for guests at a wedding ceremony to sport lengths of broad blue ribbon binding sprigs of rosemary — the plant associated with remembrance. Such favours were known as 'bride-laces'. In the early 1500s it was common for a bride-lace to be tied around one's arm but the fashion changed over the succeeding years. In his book, *A Woman Killed with Kindness* (1603), Thomas Heywood referred to a wedding party 'with nosegay and bride-laces in their hats'.

Bridegroom

Etymologists have followed the word 'bride' back via Old English to what is thought to be its Germanic origin meaning 'woman being married', but they have had little equal success with the word 'groom'. It pops up in Middle English as a synonym for boy or male servant, and the idea that a groom was someone who took care of horses did not develop until the seventeenth century. Instead it is thought that the word 'bridegroom' is a fourteenth-century adaptation of *brydguma*, literally 'bride man' but no one is sure quite why. Certainly in many parts of Europe it was customary for the newly married man to serve his new wife at their wedding feast and the conjecture is that on such an occasion, as he was acting as a servant, he should be called the bride's groom. It is claimed that the term eventually became bridegroom.

Bridewell

This pretty word has nothing at all to do with brides or good fortune but was the generic name for a prison or place of detention. The original Bridewell was a medieval palace built near St Bridget's or St Bride's Well in London. It was rebuilt by Henry VIII and eventually handed over by his son, Edward VI, to the city of London to be used as a House of Correction. Damaged during the Great Fire of London, Bridewell was rebuilt again and the name spread around the country as a term for similar institutions where vagrants and vagabonds could be corrected by whipping and hard labour.

Buxom

A cheerful word, buxom describes a woman of ample frame and bust, and has done so since the sixteenth century. But buxom has not always been so straightforward. Indeed originally it meant 'obedient or compliant' and in the twelfth century members of both sexes were advised to be 'buxom toward God'. From there the word developed to mean 'flexible', and even later was used to describe someone who was 'easy-going and jolly'. From there it was short leap for buxom to be used as an adjective meaning 'healthily plump and vigorous'. It was at that point men ceased to be described as 'buxom' and the word became distinctly feminine.

Caesar's Wife

The full expression is 'Caesar's wife must be above suspicion', and was his own response when asked to defend why he divorced his second wife, Pompeia, in 61BC. He did so after a furore in his household during the celebrations of the sacred rituals to Bona Dea, the good goddess. The goddess was considered so chaste and virtuous that homage to her could only be paid by women and at night. So as not to offend the goddess even sculptures or paintings of men had to be draped during the ceremonies. Pompeia and the leading ladies of Rome gathered for the ritual but shortly after it began there was a hullabaloo and one of the celebrants, dressed in woman's clothing, was revealed to be a man called Publius Clodius, a renowned womaniser who was intent on seducing Pompeia. The resultant public outcry led Caesar to divorce his wife, not because he believed her guilty of impropriety but because he considered she should not be considered even capable of causing offence. The term came into English in the mid-sixteenth century following the publication of an English translation of Plutarch's *Lives*.

Calamity Jane

Any woman who appears to court disaster or always looks on the dark side is called a 'Calamity Jane'. The reference is to the stage name of Martha Jane Canary who was born in Deadwood, South Dakota in 1852. There are various tales about her, many at odds, but the consistent theme is that she was a fearsome shot who threatened 'calamity' to any man who upset her. Having been a cowboy, a gold prospector, a bullwhacker and an Indian fighter she eventually took her sharp-shooting skills onto the stage. It is claimed that eleven of her twelve husbands died untimely deaths and she, herself, was supposedly renowned for being unlucky and bringing misfortune to bear on her associates.

Call Me Madam

This flippant response to the question of how one should be addressed comes from the reply of the first American woman to be appointed to a cabinet position. In 1933 Frances Perkins was appointed Secretary of Labour by President Roosevelt. When asked by a group of reporters after her first meeting how she should be addressed she is said to have replied 'Call me Madam'. The expression was later used by Irving Berlin as a title for a Broadway musical, starring Ethel Merman, which told the story of a female ambassador appointed to represent the United States in an unheard-of European country.

Calliope

Quite how an instrument that is based on a set of steam whistles and a keyboard was granted the name of the chief of the Nine Muses has never been fully explained. But maybe to those who loved the extraordinary sound associated with nineteenth-century steam boats and circuses it was appropriate, as Calliope in Greek means 'beautiful voice'. In mythology she was the goddess of epic poetry said to inspire eloquence. As an aside, Calliope was one of the nine daughters of Zeus and Mnemosyne who between them took charge of the liberal arts. Her sisters were Clio (history), Erato (love poetry), Euterpe (music and lyric poetry), Melpomene (tragedy), Polyhymnia (hymns and mime), Terpsichore (dance and choral song), Thalia (comedy and pastoral poetry) and Urania (astronomy). Know collectively as 'The Muses' they were the origin of the word 'museum', a place of learning and arts.

Cat And Mouse Act

This was the popular name of an Act of Parliament passed in 1913 as a direct result of the women's suffrage movement. The Prisoners

(Temporary Discharge for Ill Health) Act allowed for prisoners to be released on licence and re-imprisoned when and if the need arose. It was designed to stop women going on hunger strike in the cells and in so doing being heralded as martyrs to the cause. The fight for women to be given the vote was particularly militant between 1903 and 1914 and was driven by the Women's Social and Political Union, led by Emmeline Pankhurst with the support of her daughters. Mrs Pankhurst's younger daughter, Sylvia, was imprisoned nine times under the 'Cat and Mouse' Act.

Catherine Wheel

The name given to the firework that revolves sending out showers of coloured sparks comes from the trials of St Catherine of Alexandria in the early fourth century. Legend tell us that the pagan Catherine converted to Christianity following a vision but was captured and tried for her new faith. During her trial she eloquently converted fifty philosophers, who in turn were executed by the Emperor Maxentius for their folly. Catherine was imprisoned but proceeded to convert her captors, an act which led the Emperor, who had been spurned as a husband by Catherine, to order her execution. She was to be tortured to death on a spiked wheel, but legend states that the wheel miraculously broke before it could perform its gruesome task. Nonetheless Catherine was beheaded and went on to become one of the most popular saints of the Middle Ages.

Charlie's Dead

This was a popular school expression in the 1950s to tell a girl that her petticoat or slip was showing. It is not known how the saying came into being but there is much conjecture. One theory is that it refers to the white ribbons that were worn by the supporters of the Jacobite cause in the eighteenth century. With the defeat and flight of the Young Pretender, also known as Bonnie Prince Charlie, the fight was over and the need for recognition gone. Another idea is that the expression somehow relates to the execution of Charles I in 1649, and yet another that the name 'Charlie' is irrelevant, as if a slip was showing it could be said to be at 'half-mast', the recognised symbol of bereavement.

Chatelaine

This word comes directly from French and in the mid-nineteenth century was the term to describe the mistress of a country house. (Curiously, the male equivalent, chatelain, had been in use since the early sixteenth century.) In her position the lady of the house was required to keep such items as her keys, scissors and thimble-case close at hand and for that purpose it was customary to wear a clasp on the waist from which these various trinkets hung on small chains. While it is rare to hear a woman described as a chatelaine these days, the name has persisted for the brooch or clasp which she wore.

Cheesecake

In press slang, cheesecake, is the name given to photographs of girls or women used primarily for their appeal rather than their news value. The expression dates from America in the 1930s when the idea of the 'pin-up' picture was in its infancy. Soft muslin cloth would be tied over the lens of the camera to 'soften' the resultant photo and make any blemishes disappear. As the most common use of muslin at the time was as a protective covering for cheese, it is thought that is how the expression evolved.

Cinderella

The classic rags to riches story, *Cinderella* is one of the most favourite fairy stories of all time. It is thought to be of Eastern origin and ancient but its popularity was assured when it featured in Charles Perrault's *Histoires ou Contes du Temps Passé*, published in 1697. It tells the tale of a young girl who is able to go to a grand ball through the intervention of a fairy godmother. Cinderella captures the heart of the prince and he finally finds her again by means of a glass slipper that she lets slip in her rush to meet her midnight curfew. They marry and live happily ever after.

Cleopatra's Nose

This expression is used to describe how a small thing can have great consequences. It comes from a quotation by the seventeenth-century philosopher, Blaise Pascal, who said, 'If the nose of Cleopatra had been shorter, the whole face of the earth would have been changed'. The allusion is to the enormous effect her seduction of Julius Caesar and Marcus Antonius had on her position and that of her realm of Egypt. The implication is that had she been less captivating events would have taken a different course.

Cool As A Cucumber

Cucumbers have been known to maintain a cool temperature since they were first cultivated in ancient times and it may not be an accident that they were first extensively propagated in the hot climates of India and the Near East. This characteristic has led to the popular synonym 'as cool as a cucumber' when referring to someone who remains perfectly composed in all circumstances.

Cornelia's Jewels

This delightful expression refers to one's children. It alludes to Cornelia, the mother of the Gracchi, who became important statesmen in ancient Rome. Legend has it that one day Cornelia received a woman visitor who delighted in flaunting her wealth and her gems. Eventually the visitor requested to be shown Cornelia's treasures. At once Cornelia called her sons to her side and said 'These are my jewels in which alone I delight'.

Crabbing For Husbands

This is an old custom from the west of England that would take place in the autumn. Young girls would collect crab apples and lay them out in the shape of the initials of various eligible young men. On St Michaelmas Day, originally 29 September, the girls would inspect their handiwork. The initials which were best preserved were said to indicate their best prospects for a husband.

Cut A Dido

There are two explanations as to what this expression actually means. The first suggests that to 'cut a dido' means to gain advantage over an unwary opponent and it comes from the actions of the legendary Queen of Carthage when she was a young princess. It is said that when she arrived in Africa Dido made an arrangement to buy a piece of land, the size of which could be enclosed by the hide of a bull. Once the deal had been struck Dido cut the skin into one long continuous and fine strip which encircled a large area of ground – supposedly the site of her walled city of Carthage.

The second explanation is still linked to Dido but this time in connection with a ship named in her honour. In the nineteenth century HMS *Dido* gained a reputation for clever and imaginative manoeuvres as she went about her naval duties, much to the petty annoyance of the rest of the fleet. Consequently, in time to 'cut a dido' meant to 'show off'.

Dame School

For hundreds of years the only opportunity many children in Britain had to gain an education was by attending a 'dame school'. Such establishments were run by a single teacher, usually an untrained woman, as a means of providing a small income for herself. According to *The School Mistress*, published by William Shenstone in the mid-eighteenth century, every village in England boasted such a school run 'in lowly shed' by 'matron old' who 'boasts unruly brats with birch to tame'. A hundred years later, in the 1830s, it was estimated that of the one hundred and twenty-three thousand children who attended elementary school, more than forty per cent were Dame School pupils.

Damsel In Distress

Fair damsels and chivalrous knights are stuff of fairy tales, and it is thought that it is from such stories that the expression 'damsel in distress' made its way into everyday speech to describe a situation where a young woman is in difficulty. But curiously the word damsel at one time or another has been used to describe both the maid and the man. In its feminine form, 'damsel' applied to a girl of good birth who acted as a companion for the daughter of a nobleman. A particular task of a damsel was to ensure her lady was never left alone with a man. The position was much sought after as it ensured the young girl had the opportunity to be educated in the ways of an aristocratic family, and improved her chances of making a good marriage. The masculine use of 'damsel' is older, and described the son of a king, prince or nobleman before he became a knight.

Dancing Water

Any lotion, potion or cosmetic that claims to improve a woman's beauty was known as 'dancing water'. The reference is to an old French fairy tale in which 'The Dancing Water' was a waterfall in the Burning Forest. Any woman who drank from it was rejuvenated and forever beautiful.

Deb's Delight

This was a 1960s' slang term to describe a young, upper class man who might well be considered eligible by the young women of his acquaintance on account of his money and breeding rather than his intellect. 'Deb' is an abbreviation of 'debutante', which was first used in 1837 – the year Queen Victoria ascended to the throne – to describe a girl 'coming out' into society or one who is presented at court. The Buckingham Palace ritual came to an end in 1958, as part of a series of moves to modernise the monarchy, but the debutante and the 'London Season' lived on under the aegis of one of its greatest supporters, Peter Townend, formerly the social editor of *Tatler*.

Diamonds Are Forever

The name of Ian Fleming's 1956 James Bond novel is a variation of the saying, 'A diamond is forever'. Although this sounds like an old proverb, the expression was coined as a 1939 advertising campaign slogan for De Beers Consolidated Mines, one of the key companies in the diamond industry, to promote the sale of diamond engagement rings. The expression 'Diamonds are a Girl's Best Friend', on the other hand, comes from the musical, *Gentlemen Prefer Blondes*, originally produced in 1949. Carol Channing took the part of the leading lady on the stage, but Marilyn Monroe made the part her own in the 1953 film version. The most quoted line from the song, composed by Jules Styne, with lyrics by Leo Robin is: 'A kiss on the hand may be quite continental but diamonds are a girl's best friend.'

Distaff Side

A distaff was a forerunner of the spindle of a spinning wheel and in ancient times this cleft stick of about a yard long was used to wind wool or flax during the spinning process. As spinning was predominantly women's work, distaff became synonymous with female authority and the 'distaff side' was the female branch of a family. There was even a St Distaff's Day which was on January the seventh, the day after the Feast of the Epiphany – the traditional end of the Christmas festivities – when women were expected to return to their daily toil.

Dolly Varden

This was a name given to a style of dress popular with young girls in the mid-nineteenth century. It takes its name from a character in Charles Dickens' *Barnaby Rudge*, published in 1841. The character was portrayed as 'the very impersonation of good-humour and blooming beauty'. The fashion named in her honour involved flowered-print dresses tight at the waist and flower-strewn hats worn on the tilt with a bow under the chin. To be called 'a regular Dolly Varden' was a high compliment indeed for any young girl.

Don't Teach Your Grandmother To Suck Eggs

There are several variations on this very old admonition not to try to tell someone older and wiser what they might be expected to know already, and they nearly all include grandmothers. Variously it was warned that it was inadvisable to try and teach your grandmother to 'grope ducks', 'grope a goose', 'sup sour milk' or 'roast eggs' but 'suck eggs' seems to have had lasting quality. It was first referred to by Jonathan Swift in his *Polite Conversation* of 1738.

Dragon Lady

The original Dragon Lady was a cartoon character in an American comic strip. A beautiful Chinese seductress, the Dragon Lady appeared in *Terry and the Pirates*, which originated in 1934. More recently Nancy Reagan, wife of President Ronald Reagan, was given the nickname during her husband's reign in the White House during the 1980s. Far from being complimentary she was so called because of what was seen to be her rather haughty and manipulative style.

Dreaming Bread

This was the name in Yorkshire given to a small piece of wedding cake which could be used to help a girl find out whom she was fated to marry. The ritual involved passing a morsel of the cake through a wedding ring nine times and then putting the morsel under her pillow. The belief was that the girl would then dream of her future mate. What is more, if she kept the small piece of cake safely, it was thought that it would ensure her husband-to-be would be forever faithful.

Dressed To Kill

Any woman who is 'dressed to kill' is likely to be very smart, very fashion-able and in a position of bowling over a member of the opposite sex. For 'kill' you really need to read 'conquer', and while now it is said mainly of women, in times past it applied to men as well.

Duke Of Exeter's Daughter

In *The Fortunes of Nigel*, an historical novel, Sir Walter Scott has his hero say 'they threatened to make me hug the Duke of Exeter's daughter' – an embrace that would have not been heart-warming, as the Duke of Exeter's daughter was the rack. In 1420 John Holland, the Duke of Exeter, was appointed by King Henry V as Constable of the Tower of London and one of his innovations during his tenure was the introduction of one of the most feared instruments of torture.

Dumb Dora

This was an expression that was very popular in the 1920s to describe a stupid woman or a giddy young girl. Some people think it is an allusion to Dora Spenlow, the dim-witted wife of Charles Dickens' eponymous hero *David Copperfield*. If so it took a long time to catch on, as the book was published in 1850. Another suggestion is that the term stems from Britain's 'Defence of the Realm Act' (DORA), an Emergency Act brought in during World War I that many considered to be ill-conceived.

Emily's List

The Emily in question is not a real person but an acronym for *Early Money Is Like Yeast,* a group set up in America in 1985 to raise money to fund more women politicians. (There was a deliberate pun intended with the notion that yeast is the agent that makes 'dough' rise.) The group rapidly gained a reputation for being politically effective and in February 1993 Emily's List was launched in Britain. The aim is to dramatically change the gender balance at Westminster in favour of Labour women. Following the 2001 General Election a hundred and eighteen women Members of Parliament were returned: ninety-four Labour, fourteen Conservative, five Liberal Democrats and one each from the Scottish National Party, Ulster Democrat Unionist, Sinn Fein and Ulster Unionist parties.

Enola Gay

In what could be argued as an unenviable tribute, Enola Gay was the name of the American plane that dropped the atomic bomb on Hiroshima in 1945. The pilot was Colonel Paul W. Tibbets and his aircraft was named after his mother.

Face That Launched A Thousand Ships

This reference is to Helen of Troy, celebrated as the most beautiful woman in the ancient world. In Greek mythology she was the daughter of Zeus and Leda and her abduction by the Trojan prince, Paris, led to the fabled Trojan War. In Christopher Marlowe's *Doctor Faustus*, which was written in about 1594, the spirit of Helen is summoned and addressed with what have become extremely well-known lines: 'Was this the face that launch'd a thousand ships, And burnt the topless towers of Illium?' Marlowe made reference to Helen and the thousand ships again in *Tamburlaine the Great*, as did Shakespeare in his *Troilus and Cressida*.

Faint Heart Ne'er Won Fair Lady

This old proverb, which suggests that courage is essential if you wish to win the affections of your heart's desire, was first known in its modern form in the early seventeenth century. Earlier versions of the proverb, which is thought to date back to around 1390, have the word 'castle' rather than 'lady'. Then in 1580, in *Euphues And His England*, written by John Lyly, both terms were combined: 'Faint hart Philautus, neither winneth Castell nor Lady'. Suffice to say that the 'lady' element of the expression appears to have won supremacy and by 1605 William Camden wrote in *Remains*: 'Faint heart never wonne fair lady'.

Fairy Godmother

Any woman who causes something exciting or extraordinary to happen to someone else can be dubbed a 'fairy godmother'. The allusion is to the agent of good in the fairy story of *Cinderella*, but there are many other ancient tales where fairies save the day. They nearly always take human form but are usually very small – in contrast to the enormity of their magical powers.

Fashion Victim

If, in your attempts to keep up with the trends of the day, you pay scant regard to whether or not particular items of clothing suit you – then you could justifiably be called a 'fashion victim'. It is a term most commonly used to describe women and it is thought it originates from the 1970s and its use in the American journal, *Womens Wear Daily*.

Female

The structure of the word often leads to the notion that the word 'female' is somehow a derivation of the word 'male', so it will please feminists to know that is not the case at all. 'Female' stems from the French *femelle,* which in turn comes from the Latin *femella*, the diminutive form of *femina,* meaning 'woman'. The English word 'male' followed a similar route via the French *masle*, but the stem is the Latin *masculus*. It was in the fourteenth century that the spelling of what was then 'femele' changed, probably because of the similarity of the sound of the two opposite words and their obvious association.

Female Of The Species

The expression is the title of a 1911 poem by Rudyard Kipling. It puts forward the argument that women, because of their role as mothers, need to be, and are, 'more deadly than the male'. But while the line is often quoted, the ending of the poem is less well known than perhaps it ought to be:

And Man knows it! Knows, moreover, that the Woman that God gave him.
Must command but may not govern – shall enthral but not enslave him.
And *She* knows, because *She* warns him, and Her instincts never fail,
That the Female of Her Species is more deadly than the Male.

Femme Fatale

It is difficult to pinpoint exactly when this expression was adopted into English directly from French, but certainly the type of woman to whom it refers is generally considered to be as old as time itself. A 'femme fatale' is a woman who uses her charm and seductive qualities to lead men where they may not necessarily wish to go. The list of women considered to be worthy of the title throughout history probably begins with Eve in the Garden of Eden, but the femme fatale is still much in evidence today as an identifiable character in literature, films and real life.

Finished To The Fingernail

Anything or anyone to whom this expression is applied would be immaculate and perfect in every detail. The allusion is that good grooming extends to the extremities and a manicured hand demands attention. Historically such attention would have involved filing and shaping the nails and perhaps even tinting them with red, scented oil before buffing them with a chamois cloth. It was not until 1925 that nail polish was invented and manicures took on a whole new dimension.

For Better Or Worse

Part of the traditional Church of England wedding vows were extended in Australia in the 1940s, at least in common parlance. It was commonly said by women whose husbands had retired, often a testing time in a marriage, that 'I married him for better or worse, but please God, not for lunch'.

Frills And Furbelows

Anything showy, ostentatious or superfluous can be dismissed as being all 'frills and furbelows', but originally a furbelow was simply a gathered flounce on a woman's skirt or petticoat. The word comes from the Spanish, *falbala*, and it came into English in the eighteenth century along with the fashion.

Frou-frou

The French devised this word, which came across the Channel in the mid-nineteenth century, to describe the rustling noise made by a woman's skirt, especially a skirt made of silk. In England it was used to describe any kind of elaborate decoration or ornamentation on a woman's dress. In more modern times it is used to describe anything that is particularly frilly or 'girly', as in a quotation from Max Shulman's 1951 book, *Dobie Gillis*, 'Is that what you want in a girl – chi-chi, frou-frou, fancy clothes, permanent waves?'.

Gaiety Girl

A general term to describe a chorus girl or non-classical dancer, the term comes from the Gaiety Theatre, a popular place of entertainment in Victorian London. The range of its performances varied, but the Gaiety tended to favour comedy and burlesque.

Gamp

Charles Dickens' nurse in *Martin Chuzzlewit* is considered by many to be one of his finest comic characters. Apart from being rather partial to gin, Sarah Gamp was also fearful of a sudden downpour and always carried a large umbrella. The popularity of the book in 1844 and the public enthusiasm for Sarah Gamp, led to her surname becoming a slang term for an umbrella.

Giaconda Smile

Also known in France as 'La Giaconda', Leonardo da Vinci's masterpiece 'Mona Lisa' is particularly famous for the subject's enigmatic smile. Painted around 1503, the 'Mona Lisa' has fascinated experts for centuries and there has been much debate as to not only who the Mona Lisa was, but also what it was that inspired her secretive smile. Anyone who responds equally mysteriously to a question can be said to give a 'Giaconda' or a 'Mona Lisa' smile, as in 'She declined to express an opinion, answering only with a Mona Lisa smile', A.S. Byatt, *Possession*, 1990.

Gibson Girl

At the end of the nineteenth century and the beginning of the twentieth, a 'Gibson Girl' became shorthand for describing the ideal woman who was beautiful, well-groomed and wasp-waisted. The expression originated with an American illustrator, Charles Dana Gibson, whose pen and ink drawings of elegant women featured in a number of magazines and novels. Gibson's drawings had a great influence on the fashion of the day and promoted the idea that well-bred and beautiful women were equally at home riding a bicycle or on a tennis court as they were dancing the night away or playing hostess at elegant dinners. With the advent of the flapper era, the 'Gibson Girl' began to look old-fashioned and out of kilter and her creator quietly turned his attention to other artistic pursuits. However, her name reappeared many years later when the hand-cranked radio transmitters on life rafts were nick-named 'Gibson Girls' by American forces because of their shape.

Girls Will Be Girls

While it must have been known since time immemorial that girls have a certain predisposition to being mischievous and fun-loving, the expression 'girls will be girls' seems to date from 1894. It was used in *The Dolly Dialogues*, a series of sketches of the London season, by the novelist Sir Anthony Hope Hawkins (known as Anthony Hope). The sketches were published in the *Westminster Gazette*, and the sixteenth included the lines: 'Boys will be boys –', 'And even that . . . wouldn't matter if we could only prevent girls from being girls'. One suspects that Anthony Hope was drawing on ancient wisdom for inspiration.

Give One The Mitten

This was a euphemism for discarding a lover or sweetheart. It has been suggested that the term is a witty variation of the Latin word, *mittere*, meaning to send or dismiss.

Giving The Cold Shoulder

The original cold shoulder in this well-used turn of phrase was a rather bland cold shoulder of mutton, which a host would produce for a guest who had outstayed his welcome. On arrival the guest would have been treated to a tasty, hot, roast joint; the cold shoulder, by contrast, was less appealing and a none too subtle sign that it was time to leave. The meaning has subsequently extended beyond the code of hospitality. In its wider sense, 'giving the cold shoulder' means 'assuming a distant manner' which makes it clear that you want nothing to do with a particular individual.

Goldilocks

The central character in a well-known children's story took her name from a term that has been used for blonde, curly headed children for hundreds of years. 'Goldilocks' has been used as a pet name since the sixteenth century when it was predominantly used in relation to young girls and women. In contrast, it is thought that the story of *Goldilocks and the Three Bears* is much younger, and in its earliest versions there was no sign of 'Goldilocks' at all. Instead the intruder was either an old woman or a fox. Then in 1849 Joseph Cundall's version of the story in *Treasury of Pleasure Books for Young Children* featured a little girl called 'Silver Hair'. Nine years later, in *Aunt Mavor's Nursery Tales*, the character was called 'Silver-Locks' and ten years after that in 1868, in *Aunt Friendly's Nursery Book*, she became 'Golden Hair.' It was not until 1904 in a book called *Old Nursery Stories and Rhymes* that she finally became 'Goldilocks'.

Gossip

There is a modern, anonymous, saying, 'I never repeat gossip – so listen carefully', but the origin of the word 'gossip' goes back a very long way indeed. It comes from *godsib,* an Old English term for 'a sponsor at baptism'. By the fourteenth century the use of the word *godsib* had broadened to include any friend or acquaintance. However, over the next two hundred years the word transformed into 'gossip' and took on the meaning we know today – that of idle talk, usually about other people's affairs, or a name for any person who indulges in such tattle.

Granny Knot

A nautical expression for a reef knot that is not tied the correct way, 'right over left, left over right', and consequently is liable to slip. 'Granny' is the seventeenth century version of *grannam*, the colloquial form of *grandam*, 'a grandmother or old woman'. The implication is that fingers that have lost their agility, and minds no longer keen, can be fuddled when it comes to the task of tying a simple knot.

Granny Smith

The popular, distinctively green, dessert apple is named after the woman who first cultivated it in the mid-nineteenth century. Maria Ann Smith was a gardener in New South Wales, Australia, and her apple is thought to be a derivation of a type of French crab apple.

Grass Widow

We tend to think of a 'grass widow' these days as a woman who is left alone for long periods of time while her husband follows his own pursuits – but originally it meant something quite different. A 'grass widow' in the sixteenth century referred to a woman who had lived with several men, whether or not she had bothered to marry them. (It has been suggested that the 'grass' alluded to lying in fields rather than in a marital bed.) In the nineteenth century the expression took on a different meaning and was used to describe the European women in British India who were sent by their husbands to the cooler climes in the green hills during the heat of the summer. The term is used in John Lang's *Wanderings in India*, published in 1859: 'Grass widows in the hills are always writing to their husbands, when you drop in upon them'.

Grow Like Topsy

Anyone or anything that grows at a seemingly rapid rate can be said to 'grow like Topsy'. The allusion is to a character in Harriet Beecher Stow's novel of 1852, *Uncle Tom's Cabin*. In it there is a mischievous little orphan called Topsy, who when asked where she came from replied, 'I spect I grow'd. Don't think nobody never made me'.

Hand That Rocks The Cradle

This tribute to maternal power is a partial quotation from a poem written in the nineteenth century by an American, William Ross Wallace, called *What Rules the World?* The opening line is, 'They say that Man is mighty', but the poem concludes with:

> But a mightier power and stronger
> Man from his throne has hurled.
> And the hand that rocks the cradle
> Is the hand that rules the world.

Harlot

This is one example of many negative words in English that originally applied to men but which, over the centuries, has changed its focus. In thirteenth-century England a 'harlot' was a 'young male rogue of slovenly habits' and Chaucer used it in its masculine sense, when in the *Prologue to the Canterbury Tales* he described the Summoner as 'a gentil harlot and a kynde, A better felawe sholde men nought fynde'. A hundred years later the term was being applied to both sexes, 'hordome and harloty' being a common expression used to describe the crimes of vagabond women. In the seventeenth century the term 'harlot' was en route to becoming synonymous with 'woman of ill repute' and it has been suggested that the change is somehow associated with the popular idea at the time that the word was linked to William the Conqueror's mother. Her name was *Arlette*, and because she was not married to his father Robert, William's original title was 'The Bastard'.

House-Dove

Any young girl or woman who, in the sixteenth century, preferred the warmth of her own hearth and the amusement of home to venturing out into society was known as a 'house-dove'.

Housemaid's Knee

The painful condition, bursitis, is the inflammation of the knee *bursa*, a flattened sac that separates the patella, or knee cap, from the skin. The ailment is known as 'housemaid's knee' as it is a common affliction in those who spend a lot of time kneeling. Traditionally one of the housemaid's tasks was the scrubbing and polishing of floors and that demanded a great deal of time spent on all fours.

Hussy

These days this rather derogatory term is often associated with youth, as in the expression 'young hussy', although in the sixteenth century it was simply an abbreviation of *huswife*, an early spelling of 'housewife'. According to the *Oxford English Dictionary* 'hussy' can be used to describe either 'a light or worthless woman; an ill-behaved or mischievous girl; a jade, a minx'.

i

I Want To Be Alone

This frequently quoted catchphrase belongs to the Swedish-born actress, Greta Garbo, although she always denied saying it in real life. She did use the expression in her 1932 film *Grand Hotel*, and she is quoted as begging reporters 'Why don't you let me alone'. But the myth has survived perhaps because when Garbo retired in 1941 she went on to live a secluded and reclusive life up until her death in 1990.

Iron Lady

A Soviet Defence Ministry newspaper is credited with giving the nickname 'Iron Lady' to Margaret Thatcher, Britain's longest serving Prime Minster in

150 years, and the first woman to hold the post. In 1976, three years before becoming Prime Minister, she made a speech accusing the Russians of being 'bent on world dominance'. In reply the *Red Star* published an article saying that the 'Iron Lady' was looking to revive the Cold War, suggesting, erroneously, that was the nickname by which Mrs Thatcher was known in Britain at the time.

Isabelle Yellow

This particular colour has been likened to that of old calico, a dull creamy gold. It takes its name from Isabel of Austria, who at the siege of Ostend vowed not to change her linen until the city was taken. In reality the siege lasted from 1601 to 1604. One can only assume that it must have been with a happy heart that Isabel finally replaced her shift, the colour of which had changed dramatically from three years constant wear. A similar story is also attributed to Isabel of Castile and the siege of Granada, which lasted even longer. But whichever Isabel it was, the colour 'Isabelle' became commonly recognised — so much so that in France a yellow-dun coloured horse is known as *un cheval isabelle*.

It Girl

Many attractive young women who party among the upper echelons of society are tagged as 'It Girls', but the original 'It Girl' was the actress Clara Bow (1905–1965). The popular star appeared in the 1928 film *It*, based on an Elinor Glyn story of the same name. On the billboards used to promote the film, *It* was used as the word to describe Miss Bow's electrifying sex appeal. To qualify as an 'It Girl' in modern society, a young woman must also be stylish, sexy and enjoy good social connections.

It's A Case Of January And May

When an older man marries a considerably younger woman it is some-times said that 'it's a case of January and May'. The reference is to the *Merchant's Tale* in Chaucer's *Canterbury Tales*, in which a sixty-year-old Lombard baron named January marries a pretty young maid called May.

It's Snowing Down Below

It is claimed that this is a New Zealand expression dating from the 1930s said by one girl or woman to another to advise her that her slip was show-ing. However, the contemporary British version was 'It's snowing down south'. As petticoats tended to be white, the allusion is obvious. Less obvi-ous, and unexplained, is another variation of the expression which was familiar to some Oxford schoolgirls in the 1960s, 'It's snowing in Paris'. The demise of the petticoat has rendered the expressions obsolete, and in fact the petticoat has been removed from the Retail Price Index for the first time since 1956. (The RPI is compiled by the Department of Employment to show the fluctuations in consumer prices of more than a hundred and twenty thousand items.)

Jane Doe

The female version of John Doe, the name is used in the United States when the name of the real person who is guilty of an offence is unknown, for an unidentified corpse or when, for legal reasons, the true name of a defendant cannot be given. The first use of John Doe dates from the time of the Magna Carta in 1215 which required that two witnesses needed to be produced for certain legal actions to proceed. When genuine witnesses could not be traced, the names of John Doe and Richard Doe were often used instead. In Britain the use of both names was effectively abolished by the Common Law Procedures Act of 1852, but in America the use of John Doe and his female counterpart, Jane, persists.

Jezebel

A former queen of Israel, Jezebel's name is used to describe a scheming woman, or a 'painted Jezebel' is one who uses too much make-up as a tool of seduction. The original Jezebel was married to Ahab, the King of Israel, and was blamed for introducing the worship of the Canaanite god, Baal, at the expense of the Hebrew god. A strong-willed and unforgiving woman she also had a reputation for her use of cosmetics. In the Bible in II Kings 9: 30 it says: 'And when Jehu was come to Jezreel, Jezebel heard of it: and she painted her face, and tired her head, and looked out at a window'. It was to be her last defiant act, as shortly thereafter she was thrown out of the window by her own eunuchs and trampled underfoot by the afore-mentioned Jehu.

Jolly Hockey Sticks

Said to describe a certain sort of 'gal', who is enthusiastic, sporty and generally privately educated, 'jolly hockeysticks' was coined by the British actress, Beryl Reid when she starred in the highly popular 1950s' radio programme, *Educating Archie*. For a time Miss Reid played the part of Monica, Archie's upper-class schoolgirl friend, and she claims that she came up with the expression, initially, as an exclamation.

Jumping Over The Broomstick

There are several variations on what to 'jump over the broomstick' means, depending on where it is said, but nowadays the common usage is to describe an informal and quiet wedding. The custom of literally jumping over a broomstick is associated with the traditional gypsy marriage service when the bridge and groom would hold hands and jump backwards and forwards over a broom laid on the ground. Elsewhere to 'jump over the broomstick' or sometimes 'jump over the besom' meant to forego the marriage service altogether.

June Weddings

June has long been considered a particularly auspicious month in which to get married. In mythology June is the month of Juno, the Queen of Heaven, worshipped as the goddess of marriage and childbirth. In Britain it is also fortuitous that in June the weather is often favourable.

Just Like Mother Used To Make

Although it has been recognised for centuries that a mother's cooking is hard to beat, the use of the expression in quotation marks seems to have come about in the early part of the twentieth century, when it was used as an advertising slogan by the New England Mincemeat company. To say that any food is 'just like mother used to make' is generally considered to be a compliment.

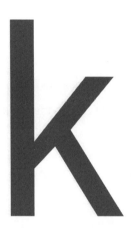

Kiss And Make It Better

A common phrase used by mothers to soothe an injured child mimics ancient sorcery, according to author and journalist, the late Edwin Radford. He asserts in *Crowther's Encyclopaedia of Phrases and Origins*, 1945, 'Sorcerers affected to kiss adder bites to make them better. It usually resulted that way – because the kissing was, in fact, a sucking out of the adder's poison!'

Kiss The Mistress

Far from being an encouragement to a man to embrace a lady, this expression comes from bowls. In former times the jack was known as 'the mistress', and when one ball glances another it is said to 'kiss' it.

Kissed The Girls And Made Them Cry

This is part of a well-known nursery rhyme, *Georgie Porgie*. In full it runs:

Georgie Porgie, pudding and pie,

Kissed the girls and made them cry;

When the boys came out to play,

Georgie Porgie ran away.

There are various suggestions as to who the real Georgie Porgie was – including George I and Charles II. There are good grounds for suggesting George I as he was a renowned womaniser who, when he first came to England, even brought two of his favourite mistresses with him. (They soon gained the nicknames, The Maypole and The Elephant-and-Castle because of their widely disparate sizes.) However, in an earlier version of the nursery rhyme it is 'Rowley Powley, pudding and pie' who does the kissing, and Charles II's nickname was 'Old Rowley'.

Knickers

Today's knickers look nothing like the original women's garment that first earned the name. The large voluminous drawers worn at the end of the nineteenth century were nicknamed 'knickers' because their shape was similar to men's knee-length trousers favoured by Dutch settlers in America. These familiarly became known as 'knickerbockers' following the publication of Washington Irving's illustrated book *History of New York*, written under the nom de plume of Deidrich Knickerbocker.

Lace Songs

There are three main types of lace and the second, bobbin or pillow lace, began as a cottage industry in the sixteenth century in Britain. It was predominantly the work of women and children and it was common for lace-makers to get together in informal groups. Each would go about her own work but the company of others was considered beneficial. To help pass the time, and seemingly to help set the pace of the work, the women would sometimes sing. Such ditties became known as 'lace songs'.

Lady Bountiful

Used to describe a woman whose generosity and largesse has an under-tone of smugness, Lady Bountiful was originally a wealthy character in George Farquhar's 1707 comedy, *The Beaux' Strategem*.

Lady Day

The 'lady' in question is the Virgin Mary, and the day is 25 March, in commemoration of her Annunciation. It used to be known as 'St Mary's Day in Lent' to distinguish it from all the other feast days dedicated to the Virgin Mary, which could also be termed 'Lady Days'. Up until the changes in the calendar in 1752, Lady Day was the official beginning of the new year. In America 'Lady Day' was also the nickname that the famous jazz singer, Billie Holiday, was given by one of her regular accompanists, Lester Young. Otherwise known as 'First lady of the Blues', Billy Holiday died in 1959.

Lady Macbeth Strategy

The world of business takeovers is murky indeed and the term 'Lady Macbeth Strategy' belongs to it. It is the name given to the modus operandi of a company that appears to support a firm that is facing an unwanted takeover from a rival, but when the deal is done joins sides with the aggressor. The reference is to Shakespeare's Lady Macbeth who, in one of the playwright's great tragedies, offers hospitality to Duncan, the king, and then encourages her husband to assassinate him.

Lady With The Lamp

The nursing pioneer, Florence Nightingale was known as 'the lady with the lamp' following the time she spent in Scutari, in Turkey, tending soldiers who had been wounded in the Crimean War. (It is claimed that through her intervention the hospital death toll fell by forty per cent.) The name comes from her habit of inspecting the wards at night carrying a Turkish lantern – a candle inside a collapsible shade. After she died in 1910 a ballad called 'The Lady with The Lamp' became popular.

Lady-Or-Tiger Situation

This expression, used to describe a scenario with only two possible outcomes – one good, one disastrous – comes from a famous nineteenth-century short story, *The Lady or the Tiger?* by Frank Stockton. It is a love story woven around an ancient king's unusual way of dispensing justice. In the tale, prisoners are given the chance to determine their own fate by choosing to enter one of two doors. Behind one was a tiger destined to eat the prisoner, and by so doing confirm his guilt. Behind the other door was a beautiful woman. Any man who opened her door was judged to be innocent.

Last Of The Red-Hot Mamas

Said these days of a keen party girl with a racy reputation, it was originally the nickname of the bawdy songstress, Sophie Tucker. It comes from the title of one of her songs, composed by Jack Yellen in 1928.

Let One's Hair Down

It is only relatively recently that women have been free to enjoy wearing their hair loose whenever they choose. For centuries women were expected to have long hair but to wear it pinned up and constrained – hair being considered an essential and personal part of a woman's femininity. It was only in the privacy of her own home that a woman could literally let her hair down and as such the term has became synonymous with care-free and uninhibited behaviour. If someone is encouraged to 'let their hair down' these days, it is an invitation to unwind, relax and let themselves go.

Let Them Eat Cake

This is famously the response of Marie Antoinette, Louis XVI's queen, when told of the bread shortage in 1789 – in spite of the fact that there is no record of her actually saying it. The phrase does appear in Rousseau's *Confessions*, written in the 1760s but not published until twenty years later, although he does not name the 'great princess' to whom he attributes the line. It has been suggested that the expression, or variations of it, had been known in France since the thirteenth century and the supposition is that *if* Marie Antoinette did actually say it, she was not being original.

Little Black Dress

The essential item in any woman's wardrobe, the little black dress or 'lbd' has been popular since the 1920s when it was seen as the perfect wear for cocktail parties. The original was created by the French fashion legend, Coco Chanel, but the idea was rapidly taken up by other designers and their customers. The enduring appeal of the little black dress has ensured it a place in fashion history and the term is now used to describe any simple dress that is suitable for a variety of social occasions.

Little Nell

The heroine of Charles Dickens' *The Old Curiosity Shop* is considered by many to be the epitome of Victorian sentimentality. Throughout the story Little Nell struggles to look after her wayward grandfather and to save both of them from a catalogue of disasters. Before she can succeed, her strength fades and she dies a lingering death. The novel was first published in weekly instalments between April 1840 and February 1841 and there are reports that 6,000 devotees, anxiously awaiting the final instalment to arrive in New York, rushed to the docks to beg sailors arriving from England to tell them of Little Nell's fate. The young heroine's plight caused equal anxiety in England and it is said that there was widespread mourning among Dickens' readers when the story ended.

Little Orphan Annie

A whole industry has built up around this irrepressible heroine of one of the longest-running American strip cartoons, originally created by Harold Gray in the 1930s for the *Chicago Tribune*. 'Little Orphan Annie' tells the story of a wild little redhead and her dog, Sandy, who are taken in by a millionaire to lead a full and exciting life of adventure. The story has since been turned into a film and a successful musical. When Harold Gray died in 1968, other artists took on the task of keeping 'Little Orphan Annie' fans happy until 1974 when the original strips were offered for syndication. Today 'Little Orphan Annie' still appears in more than a hundred and fifty daily newspapers across America.

Loathly Lady

Any woman so-called is one who has been transformed by love. The expression is thought to come from *Sir Gawain and the Green Knight,* a fourteenth-century romantic verse of unknown authorship. The 'Loathly Lady' of the story is so hideous and ugly that no one will marry her except for the gallant Gawain. Immediately after the ceremony, the hag turns into a beautiful young maid and tells how she had been bewitched. The moral of the story is that loves makes all things beautiful.

Lorelei

A fascinating woman or a siren is known as a Lorelei, even though in Germanic folklore it describes the home of a particular temptress rather than being the name of the woman herself. The Lorelei is a steep rock on the Rhine where sits a beautiful blonde siren who lures boatmen to their death through the sweetness of her song.

Lucy Stoner

In the United States, a 'Lucy Stoner' is a woman who keeps her maiden name after marriage. It alludes to an active women's rights campaigner of the mid-nineteenth century called Lucy Stone, who defied tradition, and her father, and put herself through college. When she was thirty-eight she married a like-minded man called Henry Blackwell, and on their wedding day they issued a public statement. In it they set out their convictions that marriage should not diminish a woman's rights to be an 'independent, rational being' nor should the state 'confer upon the husband an injurious and unnatural superiority'. To emphasise the point Lucy Stone used her maiden name for her entire life.

Madeleine

This small, delicate sponge cake, made famous by French author Marcel Proust in his celebrated work *À La Recherche du Temps Perdu*, takes its name from its inventor, a nineteenth-century French pastry-chef called Madeleine Paulmier. In France a 'madeleine' is traditionally baked in a scallop-shaped mould, but in England it is baked in a 'dariole' mould which is small and narrow with sloping sides. Proust was particularly fond of the delicacies and made several references to madeleines in his work, including, *'I raised to my lips a spoonful of the cake . . . a shudder ran through my whole body and I stopped, intent upon the extraordinary changes that were taking place.'*

Madrigal

The word madrigal is generally deemed to be as delightful as the thing it describes – a love or pastoral poem set to music, usually sung in part form – but there is debate as to its origin. The most commonly held theory is that it stems from the Latin, *matricalis,* meaning 'of the womb', but why is another matter altogether. There are four common explanations. The first is that the allusion is to the fact that madrigals were written in the vernacular, or 'Mother Tongue', not in the language of the church. The second holds that, even though written in the vernacular, madrigal form had its base in the 'Mother Church'. The third proposes there is a connection to the Medieval Latin word, *matricale,* meaning simple or primitive, and that because madrigals are of such simple construction that they could indeed be 'fresh from the womb'. The fourth highlights the fact that madrigals are reminiscent of a mother's affectionate song to her children, and the apparent link to the Italian word for mother, *madre.*

Mae West

The inflatable life jackets issued to the forces during World War II were named after the mistress of verbal innuendo and famously curvaceous vaudeville, stage and film star, Mae West. The allusion is to the celebrated buxom allure of the actress.

Maid Of Honour

This small tart filled with flavoured milk curd is considered to be one of the historic dishes of England. It originated in the court of Henry VIII at Hampton Court Palace, and was a particular favourite with the Queen's Maids of Honour. During the reign of George I, one particular lady's maid shared the recipe, which had until then been a closely-guarded secret, with a baker in Richmond and the tarts are still made there to this day.

Maid Of Orleans

This rather gentle title for St Joan of Arc belies the ardour, skill and tenacity of one of the most celebrated and controversial of French heroines. Born in 1412 in rural Lorraine, Joan became convinced that God needed her help to expel the English from French soil. She ended up playing a crucial role in what is now known as The Hundred Years' War, and is remembered especially for raising the siege of Orleans. Her intervention helped the dauphin, Charles, reclaim the French Crown. However, Joan was later captured and betrayed to the enemy. She died an ignominious and unjust death at the hands of the English, supported by a tribunal of French ecclesiastics. She was burned at the stake for witchcraft and heresy on 13 May 1431 in Rouen. She was finally canonised in 1920.

Marianne

In England we have 'John Bull', the United States have 'Uncle Sam', and in France 'Marianne' is the embodiment of the French Republic. She is said to represent the essential values of 'Liberty, Equality and Fraternity' and her name was also a slang term for the guillotine. Her roots are in ancient Rome, where Democracy was represented as having a woman's face. After the French Revolution there were a number of sculptures and paintings which continued the theme, using female figures to represent the values of the revolution itself. In 1792 the new republic decided that the 'state seal was to be changed and should henceforth bear the figure of France in the guise of a woman dressed after the fashion of Antiquity, standing upright, her right hand holding a pikestaff surmounted by a Phrygian bonnet, or Liberty bonnet, and her left hand resting on a bundle of arms: at her feet, a tiller.' Despite a chequered history over the ensuing centuries, Marianne has finally regained her position, and a bust of her is part of the official furnishings of every town hall in France. As for the name – it is thought that 'Marianne' was simply the name of the first model who sat for the busts. In recent years the most popular versions have been modelled on the actresses Brigitte Bardot and Catherine Deneuve. In 2003 a French television chat show host, Evelyne Thomas, was chosen to be the latest Marianne.

Martha

The name of the sister of Mary Magdalen and Lazarus has become the nickname for a conscientious housewife. St Martha, as she became, is indeed the patron saint of good housewives and in the Bible is said to be 'cumbered about much serving' (Luke 10: 38–42). In art St Martha is often depicted wearing plain, homely clothes with a bunch of keys on her girdle and sometimes seen with the dragon she is reputed to have conquered by spraying it with holy water. One can only marvel at the fore-sight of the mother of Martha Stewart, the famous domestic guru in the United States, when it came to choosing a name for her daughter.

Mary Jane Cookies

Mary Jane is the literal translation of the Spanish word, *marijuana*, a type of hemp with a strong narcotic effect. There is no definitive explanation as to why the plant should have been given two girls' names, but the transla-tion, Mary Jane, is a term for cannabis that became popular during the 1920s. Mary Jane cookies are any biscuits that include the drug as an ingredient. A famous recipe for Mary Jane Cookies appears in the *Alice B. Toklas Cookbook,* which was popular in the 1960s. In reality, however, the book had little to do with Alice B. Toklas, who was the secretary and lover of the American writer, Gertrude Stein, in Paris during the 1930s.

Mary Poppins

Anyone who is described as being a bit of a 'Mary Poppins' is in danger of being almost too wholesome and cheerful for her own good. The reference is to P. L. Travers' heroine, a nanny with magical powers, in a series of children's books. The 1964 musical film version of *Mary Poppins*, starring Julie Andrews, is considered to be a classic.

Mata Hari

A term to describe a beautiful and mysterious woman, Mata Hari was the stage name of the exotic dancer, courtesan and supposed spy, Margaretha Geetruida Zelle. She was born in Holland in 1876 and married a Dutch soldier when she was just seventeen. When the marriage failed she returned from their posting in Sumatra and became a professional 'oriental dancer' in Paris. Historians are still unsure of the role she played, but it is thought that she worked as a spy during World War I for both the French and the Germans. She was arrested and tried for espionage by a French court, who disbelieved her claim that she was a French double agent. Mata Hari was executed by firing squad on 17 October 1917.

Matilda

As anyone who is familiar with the work of Hilaire Belloc will tell you, the last thing you want to be known as is a 'Matilda'. She was one of the main characters in his *Cautionary Tales*, written in 1907:

> Matilda told such Dreadful Lies,
>
> It made one Gasp and Stretch one's Eyes.

As you might expect the young lady got her comeuppance, albeit a rather permanent one, but her name lives on as a way of describing someone who is unacquainted with the truth.

Maudlin

The English word meaning 'mawkishly emotional' or 'tearfully sentimental' comes from the name of St Mary Magdalen, the prostitute who was forgiven and saved by Jesus Christ. In early religious works, Mary Magdalen was often portrayed weeping copiously for her previous sins and her joy at redemption. The association between her and tears became fixed. Our word came via the French, *Maudelen*, the French variation of the saint's name, and was used to describe anyone who was prone to copious weeping. The change of spelling and the use of the lower case occurred in the sixteenth century.

Meddlesome Matty

Anyone so called has a tendency to get involved in things which are not really their concern. The reference is to a character in *Original Poems for Infant Minds by Several Young Persons*, a collection of children's poetry by Ann and Jane Taylor published in two volumes in 1804 and 1805. The poem, *Meddlesome Matty*, written by Ann Taylor, begins:

> One ugly trick has often spoil'd
> The sweetest and the best;
> Matilda, though a pleasant child,
> One ugly trick possess'd,
> Which, like a cloud before the skies,
> Hid all her better qualities.

The popularity of the poem meant that the term was soon used as a general expression for anyone who dabbled in other people's affairs.

Melba Toast

The Australian soprano, Helen Porter Mitchell, is better known as Dame Nellie Melba – one of the most popular opera singers of the late nineteenth and early twentieth centuries. She was acclaimed for her beauty and her talent, and among her many admirers was George Auguste Escoffier, head chef at the Savoy Hotel in London. Whenever Dame Nellie stayed at the Savoy, it is said that Escoffier delighted in preparing delicacies for her. However, the diva battled with her weight and often requested plain toast instead of elaborate meals. One day she was presented with toast that had been sliced too thinly and was overdone. Far from being annoyed she amazed Escoffier by asking if her toast could, from then on, be prepared in such a fashion. Consequently such crisp, dry slices of toast have taken her name.

Midwife

This simple word has aroused much curiosity over the years as to its origins. The answer is straightforward. 'Mid' is the Anglo Saxon word for 'with', and 'wife' was a general term for 'woman'. Hence a midwife is someone who is with a woman during childbirth, literally a 'with woman'. As an aside, the great philosopher, Socrates, is known as the 'midwife of men's thoughts', a title, it is believed, he gave himself.

Mills And Boon

Any story that is deemed to be especially romantic or tells of a couple that have surmounted all odds to be together, can be described as 'Mills and Boon'. It alludes to a London publishing house, the name of which is synonymous with escapist, sentimental romance. The company was founded in 1908 by Gerald Mills and Charles Boon and originally published a range of fiction until the 1930s when it began to specialise. The essential ingredients of a Mills and Boon romance are true love and a happy ending. The company is now owned by the Canadian-based Torstar group and publishes more than six hundred titles a year.

Miss Goody Two Shoes

A symbol of self-righteousness and affected goodness, Little Goody Two Shoes was a character in an eighteenth-century moralistic nursery story, attributed to Oliver Goldsmith. In the tale, the heroine, Margery, had only one shoe. When given another by a benefactor she ran around showing them off excitedly exclaiming 'Two Shoes'. So equipped, Margery goes on to become a teacher, happy and ready to provide good advice to all, and eventually marries a wealthy widower. Quite why her name is used in the way it is, has never been fully explained.

Miss World Order

A list that is put in reverse order, is known as being in 'Miss World order'. The expression alludes to the way the announcement is made in the international beauty contest, with the names of the runners-up being announced first. It is thought that Eric Morley, who began the competition in 1951, started the trend. When it came to the grande finale, he would always say 'I'll give you the results in reverse order'.

Mitford Funeral

Jessica Mitford, one of the six celebrated daughters of Lord Redesdale, is responsible for this expression becoming common parlance in the United States. Primarily known in Britain for her autobiographical *Hons and Rebs*, published in 1960, across the Atlantic she is renowned for the book she wrote three years later, *The American Way of Death*, an exposé of the funeral industry. The book resulted in many people opting for less elaborate and cheaper funerals. Consequently people who now do so are said to have chosen a 'Mitford funeral'.

Moaning Minnie

There is a misconception that this phrase is somehow feminine in origin, in fact it is unquestionably masculine. 'Minnie' was the slang name for a type of German mortar, used in World War I, a *Minenwerfer*, the shell of which made a characteristic moaning noise when fired. In World War II the name was also applied to air-raid sirens for a similar reason. These days it is used to describe anyone who constantly complains.

Mobcap

In the eighteenth and early nineteenth centuries, a woman whose hair was not yet 'dressed' often wore a simple, round, gathered cap to cover her tresses. In folklore such a cap was the favoured headwear of Queen Mab of the Fairies who, at that stage in history, was considered to be rather dishevelled and slatternly. The word 'mob' was a variation of her name and, used as a verb, meant to 'dress untidily'.

Modesty Blaise

A woman who shows great intelligence and bravery can be described as a 'Modesty Blaise'. It alludes to the heroine of a strip cartoon first published in *The Evening Standard* in 1963. The original Modesty, a retired gangster, took on the role of fighting crime and injustice with remarkable enthusiasm and success.

Mother

Etymologists will tell you that the word 'mother' is a derivation of the Old English word *modor*, and can be traced back to the ancestral Indo-European *mater*, descendants of which can be found in virtually all modern European languages. 'The Mother' is something else entirely. It was a name for hysteria, a disturbance of the nervous system, and any woman so afflicted was said to be 'mother-sick'. It was thought that, as women are more prone to the disorder than men, it was caused by a dysfunction of the uterus. The very word 'hysteria' comes from the Latin, *hystericus*, meaning 'belonging to or suffering in the womb'. 'Hysterical medicines' in the eighteenth century were no laughing matter but were those considered beneficial for diseases of the uterus.

Mother Carey's Chickens

This is the name given by sailors to the storm petrel, a small oceanic bird 'not unlike a large, square-tailed house-martin', 'Mother Carey' herself being nautical slang for the fulmar, a larger gull-like petrel with white head and breast. In France petrels are commonly known as 'the birds of our Mother St Mary', from the Latin *mater cara*, meaning 'dear mother'. The supposition is that to British sailors this sounded like 'Mother Carey' and that is how they translated the term. It is considered extremely unlucky to kill a petrel as legend says each bird contains the soul of a dead sailor. At sea, 'Mother Carey is plucking her goose' is a long-winded way of saying 'it's snowing'.

Mothers Day

The Christian festival of 'Mothering Sunday' is the fourth Sunday of Lent, so called because it was the day when apprentices and servants were traditionally given leave to go home. In America 'Mothers Day', is on the second Sunday in May and was established as such by Congress in 1941. The name was exported to Britain during the 1940s, but we remain true to the date and celebrate 'Mothers Day' in conjunction with 'Mothering Sunday'.

Mrs Beeton's Cookbook

Isabella Beeton's *The Book of Household Management* is the most famous English recipe book ever written and is considered to be one of the greatest publishing successes in history. It first came out in 1861 and sold more than 60,000 copies in its first year and nearly two million in the succeeding seven. Apart from thousands of recipes it offers an extraordinary range of advice and ideas. Writing in the *Oxford World's Classics Magazine*, Nicola Humble, the editor of the new edition of *Mrs Beeton's Book of Household Management* considers it 'encyclopaedic in its range' and 'so much more than a cookery book. It tells a story of a culture caught between the old world and the new, poised between modernity and nostalgia.' What makes the book even more extraordinary is that when it was published, Isabella Beeton was only twenty-five. What makes it tragic, is that she died four years later from an infection following the birth of her fourth child.

Mrs Grundy

Seen as 'the embodiment of public opinion' and 'an upholder of conventional morality' Mrs Grundy was an unseen, off-stage character in *Speed the Plough*, by Thomas Morton, first performed in 1798. During the play, when faced with a moral dilemma, the on-stage characters frequently ask 'What will Mrs Grundy say?' More than two hundred years later, Mrs Grundy can still be invoked when anyone asks what the reaction of the public might be to any given situation.

Mrs Malaprop

One of Richard Brinsley Sheridan's most memorable characters, Mrs Malaprop, appears in his comedy, *The Rivals*, which was first performed at Covent Garden in 1775. Sheridan based her name on the French expression, *mal à propos* meaning awkward or inappropriate, and in turn her name has given us the English word 'malapropism', the ridiculous misuse of a word. In the play Mrs Malaprop has a penchant for using the wrong word at the wrong time. Some of her most quoted mistakes are, 'No caparisons, miss, if you please'; 'a nice derangement of epitaphs'; and 'pineapple of politeness'. Sheridan's everlasting legacy to the English language lives on and many a modern 'Mrs Malaprop' continues her good work. Recently overheard was, 'man is not meant to be a monogram' – the word the speaker was looking for was, of course, 'monogamist'.

Mrs O'Leary's Cow

In America, Mrs O'Leary's Cow is an abbreviation for something that appears to be harmless yet causes a major disaster. The phrase stems from the great Chicago Fire of 1871, which killed 300 people, left more than a hundred thousand homeless and destroyed 17,500 buildings. The exact cause of the fire is unknown but it is believed that it started in a barn owned by a family named O'Leary. Journalists of the day speculated that Mrs O'Leary had left a kerosene lamp in the shed after milking her cow, and that the beast subsequently kicked it over. The story was later refuted but the belief lingered on that the fire had started in the O'Leary barn — maybe due to a cigar that had not been properly extinguished.

My Lady Nicotine

This rather affectionate term for what is now one of the greatest killers of the modern day, is attributed to the creator of the children's classic, *Peter Pan*, Sir James Barrie. At the time he certainly was not the only one to espouse the pleasures of smoking. A contemporary, Rudyard Kipling, is credited with saying, 'And a woman is only a woman but a good cigar is a Smoke'.

My Nose Itches

Modern young women need little encouragement to come forward, but in days past it was not always easy for a girl to clarify her intentions without appearing to be a 'brazen hussy'. From the eighteenth century until comparatively recent times, there was, however, an accepted code if a young woman was willing to accept a kiss. Apparently all she needed to say was, 'my nose itches'.

My Oath, Miss Weston

This is the nautical version of 'cross my heart and hope to die'– commonly said when you are trying to convince someone you are telling the truth. It was popular during the lifetime of Dame Agnes Weston, who founded a series of hostels, 'Sailors' Rests', at several naval ports, and who offered support in a variety of ways to naval men and their families. In 1892 'Sailors' Rests' were awarded the Royal Warrant and thereafter were known as 'Royal Sailors' Rests' and when Agnes Weston died in 1918, at the age of seventy-eight, she became the first woman to be buried with full naval honours. Her gravestone carries the epitaph, 'The Sailor's Friend'. Dame Weston's charity, now known simply as RSR, still continues her work.

My Old Dutch

An affectionate slang term for wife, 'My Old Dutch' was made popular by the singer and comedian Albert Chevalier, a music hall star in the early twentieth century. He sang a song about his wife, his nickname for her being, he said, because her face was like that of an old Dutch clock (although in fact 'Old Dutch' became his own nickname). 'Dutch' was also a well-known abbreviation of 'Duchess of Fife', cockney rhyming slang for wife, and following Chevalier's success the expression gained even wider popularity.

New Look

The French designer, Christian Dior, is considered to be the man behind transforming post-World War II fashion. His 1947 spring collection was dubbed the 'New Look' by *Life* magazine and at first was considered controversial. The short skirts and square shoulders of the early 1940s gave way to full, ballerina-length skirts and narrow waists. The emphasis was on femininity. Despite its critics, the fashion soon caught on, and variations of the 'New Look' remained fashionable well into the 1950s.

New Woman

In recent times there has been a lot written in the press about 'New Man', but in the late nineteenth century the darling of reporters was 'New

Woman' – a female who espoused emancipation and independence. More than a hundred years later the term is still being used, but with the added inference that a 'New Woman' is one who enjoys a successful career without jeopardising her femininity.

Niobe's Tears

It is Greek mythology that provides us with the 'personification of maternal sorrow'. Niobe was the daughter of Tantalus and wife of the King of Thebes, Amphion. In a proud and rash moment she suggested that her people should pay homage to her instead of celebrating the feast of the goddess, Leto. (The crux of her argument was that she had fourteen children, while Leto had only two.) Unfortunately for Niobe, Leto's children were Apollo, the god of archery, and Artemis, the goddess of hunting. The twins avenged their mother by slaying all fourteen of Niobe's children. Niobe wept herself to death and was turned to stone on Mount Sipylon, which is said to flow with a stream of her tears to this day.

Not Just A Pretty Face

This is an expression that gained popularity during the 1970s and the development of the Women's Liberation Movement. The catchphrase suggests that a woman can be clever and intelligent as well as attractive.

Not Over Until The Fat Lady Sings

There are several ideas as to the origin of this expression, but it is generally accepted to be late twentieth-century American and to refer to opera.
The allusion is that many opera singers, historically, were large women,
and that many operas end with an aria sung by the heroine. Hence, any
performance could not be considered over until she had sung.

Often A Bridesmaid

There was a popular music hall song in 1917 called 'Why Am I Always a Bridesmaid?' but it is thought that the origin of the expression, 'Often a bridesmaid, but never a bride' comes instead from an advertising slogan. In the early 1920s it was widely used to promote Listerine Mouthwash. In time the expression has come to be applied to someone who frequently 'plays second fiddle'.

Old Lady Of Threadneedle Street

This nickname for the Bank of England stems from a political cartoon drawn by James Gilray in 1797, after the bank announced that it would not be able to convert notes into gold. Gilray chose to depict the bank as an elderly woman crying 'Rape! Murder . . . Ruin!' as a young politician dipped into her pockets. The image of the Bank of England as a respectable matron stuck. To this day the bank is still known as 'The Old Lady of Threadneedle Street'.

Old Mother Hubbard

In the late nineteenth century 'Mother Hubbard' became rhyming slang for 'cupboard' in reference to the famous nursery rhyme. Fourteen verses of the rhyme first appeared in *The Comic Adventures of Old Mother Hubbard and Her Dog*, published in 1805. So successful was it, that more than ten thousand copies were distributed within a few months of its release, and the following year it was reprinted with a continuation and a sequel. In all there were twenty-six Mother Hubbard titles. Her creator is thought to be Sarah Catherine Martin, an early love of William IV, and Mother Hubbard is believed to be the housekeeper of Catherine's brother-in-law, John Pollexfen Bastard. Tradition has it that one day the lively Catherine was annoying John Bastard, the M. P. for Kitley in Devon, so he instructed her to 'runaway and write one of your stupid little rhymes'. The publishing success of Mother Hubbard was the result of her complying with his wishes.

Old Wives' Tale

Any story which has no basis in truth can be dismissed as 'an old wives' tale' and it has been so for centuries. The allusion is to the fanciful stories often related by older women which rely more on folklore than fact. The expression was used in 1595 by the dramatist George Peel as the title of a play, and Arnold Bennett published a novel entitled *The Old Wives' Tale*, in 1908. It tells the story of Constance and Sophia, two sisters of a prosperous family in Bursley between 1860 and 1906.

One Hour Dress

In the 1920s there was a dramatic change in fashion when the flapper era was born. Skirts went up, waists disappeared and the 'one hour dress' became the rage. It was a simple smock with squared sleeves and a short skirt and it took its name from the claim that any accomplished seamstress could make the dress in an hour. Using the same criteria, there is many a girl these days who must be wearing 'the five minute skirt'.

Outskirts

The English word 'skirt' comes from the Old English word for shirt, *scyrte*, but no one has worked out quite how the change of meaning came about. One theory is that Norman women wore an elaborate outer garment which they called a 'skirt' and, following the to-do in 1066, the word became known in England. It has been suggested that, because the straggle of buildings which grew up around most city walls were reminiscent of a skirt at a woman's feet, the term 'outskirts' came to describe the outer borders of any community.

Over The Moon

One of the best known English nursery rhymes is 'Hey Diddle Diddle' in which 'the cow jumped over the moon'. The verse first appeared in print in the mid-eighteenth century but the use of the expression 'over the moon' to convey great joy and elation is thought to be a much later invention. It is said that the family of Catherine Glynne – wife of the nineteenth-century British Liberal Prime Minister, William Gladstone – had an idiomatic language they used among themselves and that the Glynne family were the first to use the term in the way we do today. It was obviously known to a wider circle as well, as the entry in the diary of Lady Cavendish for the seventh of February 1857 includes the expression.

Page Three Girl

The term has come to describe any topless, photographic model but referred in the first place to the models who appear daily on page three of *The Sun* newspaper. In November 1969, a year after the paper had been bought by the newspaper magnate, Rupert Murdoch, the then-editor, Larry Lamb, introduced the feature. It has been a constant ever since.

Pandora's Box

Pandora, meaning 'all gifts' was the first human woman, according to Greek mythology. She was created by the order of Zeus who was enraged that man had been given the gift of fire, and his intent was far from comforting. Pandora brought from Olympus a box in which was contained all the evils of the world. When Pandora finally opened the box all the ills escaped, leaving Hope alone in the bottom. The expression is used to describe a series of disasters, or something that has the appearance of value but is really a curse.

Pavlova

This concoction of meringue, whipped cream and fruit is the centre of a long-standing dispute in the Antipodes. Australia likes to claim to be the birthplace of the dessert, as does New Zealand. However, there is no argument that it was named in honour of the Russian ballerina, Anna Matveyevna Pavlova (1881–1931), one of the greatest classical ballet exponents of all time.

Peach Melba

Another dessert which has Antipodean and artistic links is the Peach Melba, created by the celebrated chef, George Auguste Escoffier in 1892. Escoffier was a great fan of the Australian soprano, Dame Nellie Melba and, following one of her performances in Wagner's *Lohengrin*, he was inspired to create the dish in her honour. The key ingredients of a Peach Melba are vanilla ice cream, peaches and raspberry sauce.

Penelope's Web

Any project which, by design, will never be finished is known as 'Penelope's Web'. The expression comes from a cunning ploy devised by

Penelope, the wife of Ulysses. According to Homer, Penelope came up with an ingenious way of putting off suitors eager to make the most of her husband's absence at the siege of Troy. She told the men that she would choose one of them once she had completed the task of making a shroud for her father-in-law. To defer the day of reckoning, each evening Penelope would unravel her day's work.

Penny Weddings

In rural England it used to be common for all the villagers to be invited to the celebrations when a local girl was married. As it was well recognised that this could mean financial ruin for the girl's father, it was customary for the villagers to contribute towards the cost of the festivities. While the amount paid on such occasions was small, often a sixpence for an adult and a penny for a child, the contributions were gladly given and received. Such celebrations, in time, came to be known as 'Penny Weddings'.

Perfume

One of the most essentially feminine words, 'perfume' in its original form means 'through smoke'. Historically it was used to describe the fumes given off by the burning of scented logs or oils, incense in particular. The use of perfume as an adornment goes back thousands of years and in the earliest days perfumes were made from scented resins, spices, herbs and other plants. It is believed that the process of extracting the scent of flowers through distillation was discovered by an eleventh-century Arabian physician and such perfumes reached England by way of returning Crusaders. The first synthetic perfume was produced in the nineteenth century and the majority of perfumes made today, in an industry worth billions of pounds, are produced synthetically.

Perm

The common abbreviation of 'permanent wave', a 'perm' is a way of treating the hair using chemicals and heat to produce long-lasting curls and body. The method was devised in 1906 in London and was originally a long and sometimes painful process. 'Perms' came into their own post-war and are still an essential part of personal grooming for many women.

Petticoat Government

The power wielded by the woman of the household or domination by a woman who, figuratively, 'wears the trousers' is known as 'petticoat government'. But while we think of 'petticoat' as an essentially feminine garment, the original petticoats were worn by men. The name comes from the French *pety cote,* the name of a little jacket worn under a doublet or a coat of mail in the fifteenth century. Even when women took to wearing 'petticoats' they were again a type of short coat. Quite how the garment slipped down the body to become a skirt has never been fully explained but by the seventeenth century the term described both outer and under garments. It took another hundred years for the petticoat to gain its exclusive role as an underskirt.

Petticoat Tails

In Scotland 'petticoat tails' are a type of shortbread which became popular during the time of Mary, Queen of Scots. In French, Mary's first language, the biscuits were known as *petites gatelles,* meaning 'little scallops', because of their frilled edge. To the local ear the name sounded like 'petticoat tails' and as such the term has endured.

Pin Money

The provision made by a husband for his wife's personal expenditure was called 'pin money' and comes from the Middle Ages when pins were essential, but expensive, items to fasten clothes. Early pins were made of fish bones, thorn, or slivers of animal bone. Then came iron, bronze wire and later still, brass. Before the Industrial Revolution brought about mass-produced pins, it took eighteen people, each performing a different task, to make just one pin and consequently the high labour costs were reflected in the price of the final item. With the introduction of more permanent forms of fastening the original use and meaning of the term 'pin-money' lost significance. The expression lives on, however, to describe small amounts of money a wife may call her own.

Pin-Up Girl

The natural enthusiasm of the male for the female form has been responsible for countless works of art (and many that are not) since time immemorial. The Victorians had 'pin-up girls', only not known as such, and it was not until World War II that the 'pin-up girl' came into her own. There was an enormous demand from the troops for pictures of alluring and glamorous girls to brighten up their barracks and fuel their fantasies. Such photos needed to be portable and were designed to be 'pinned' to a wall rather than encased in a frame. Once the war was over the demand did not fade and pin-up art became a recognised genre, often associated with the production of calendars for the male market. If a woman was described as a 'pin-up girl' it suggested that she was very attractive and worth looking at.

Pollyanna

Anyone who is relentlessly cheerful and perpetually optimistic can be called a 'Pollyanna'. The allusion is to the heroine of a series of children's books written by the American author, Eleanor Porter, whose work was very popular at the end of the eighteenth and in the early nineteenth centuries. Porter's 'Pollyanna' was particularly fond of the 'just being glad' game, the point of which was 'to find something about everything to be glad about – no matter what 'twas'.

Poor Little Rich Girl

Originally the title of a 1912 novel by Eleanor Gates, and later a film star-ring Mary Pickford, the expression 'poor little rich girl' is most strongly associated with Gloria Vanderbilt. Heiress to an immense fortune, she was at the centre of a bitter custody battle in the 1930s, when she was only ten years old, between her widowed mother and her paternal aunt. Gloria went on to become a successful artist, actress, designer and business-woman but, true to the expression, her money was no protection against unhappiness. She has been married four times and her son, Carter, committed suicide. Other heiresses who have been dubbed 'poor little rich girls' include Christina Onassis – daughter of the shipping magnate, Aristotle Onassis – who took her own life.

Pope Joan

The name of a very popular nineteenth-century family card game, played with elaborate boards and without the eight of diamonds, alludes to a story that was once and for all confirmed as myth in 1863. In the Middle Ages it was firmly believed that a woman born in Germany to English parents went on to become the ninth-century Pope John VIII. The legend is that she disguised herself as a man, called herself Johannes Angelicus and went, first to Athens and then to Rome, to study the scriptures. Her knowledge and wisdom was such that, allegedly, she was elected to the papacy in 855. Supposedly, two years later, she went into labour during a church procession and died during childbirth. There was a resurgence of interest in Pope Joan when a novel called *Papissa Joanna* was published in 1886, but quite why the inventors of the card game decided to name it after her is not known.

Powder One's Nose

There are any number of euphemisms for going to the lavatory, and this is just one of them. The expression became fashionable in the early years of the twentieth century, when to apply make-up in public was considered vulgar in the extreme.

Power Dressing

In the 1980s there was great adherence by many women to a style known colloquially as 'Power Dressing'. That idea was that your clothes should reflect your influence and career status. Minimal jewellery, sombre colours and suits with wide-shouldered jackets were the mark of the look, which was particularly popular with businesswomen.

Pumpkin Time

This is the time when the magic ends and reality kicks in, and the expression is used to describe the end of a particularly prosperous or happy period. The allusion is to the fairy story of *Cinderella*, in which the heroine is allowed to go to the Prince's ball with the qualification that she must leave at midnight or her coach will turn back into a pumpkin and her horses into mice.

Queen Anne Is Dead

This phrase was used as a sarcastic reply to someone whom you thought was imparting stale news or information that you already knew. It was first used in a ballad in 1722, eight years after Queen Anne had died. The last of the Stuart monarchs, she was described as 'one of the smallest people ever set in a great place'. Cheerful and conscientious, Anne survived seventeen pregnancies and sixteen dead babies. Her only child to live through infancy, William Duke of Gloucester, died when he was just eleven. The Queen's death in 1714 was of great import and resulted in the crown being passed to the German Hanoverians. As a result there could have been hardly anyone in Britain who was not aware of her passing and this gave the bite to the expression, 'Queen Anne is dead'.

Queen For A Day

The expression is used to describe a woman who is treated to an experience out of keeping with her day-to-day existence. It comes from the title of a 1940s' American radio programme which offered women the opportunity to have a wish granted. Later a popular television programme adapted the idea and in 1951 there was a film of the same name.

Queen's Tobacco Pipe

The Queen was Queen Victoria and the pipe was a kiln near the London docks where smuggled goods such as tobacco, cigars and tea were burned by Customs officials. There was the belief that all contraband that was suitable for burning was fed into the furnace, but according to William Walsh's *Book of Literary Curiosities* published in 1900 the best tobacco was kept aside and 'supplied to convict prisons for the consolation of criminal lunatics'.

Queen's Weather

In Victorian times it was noted that whenever the Queen appeared in public the weather would be fine and warm, and so good weather came to be known as 'Queen's weather'. Her Majesty's ability to bring out the sunshine was obviously hereditary, as during the reign of George V (Queen Victoria's grandson) the phrase was adapted to 'King's weather', as it was noted that whenever he ventured out on matters of state or on official business the weather was also invariably good.

Rose Is A Rose

This expression, to describe something that cannot be explained but which is perfect in its own right, is from 'Sacred Emily', a poem by Gertrude Stein. The full line is, 'Rose is a rose is a rose'. Contrary to misconception, Stein was not talking about the flower but about the artist, Sir Frederick Rose, of whose work she was particularly fond.

Ruth Draper Garden

In the first half of the twentieth century Ruth Draper was considered to be the greatest exponent of the one-woman show. An American, she made her professional debut in 1920 and performed all over the world, including a

Royal Command performance at Windsor Castle before George V and Queen Mary. One of her 'monodramas', as she called them, was 'Showing the Garden', which was particularly popular in Britain. In it she was an Englishwoman taking a visitor, Mrs Guffer, on a tour of her garden. The garden was, of course, normally exquisite – but just not at that time of year. As the sketch progressed, Draper offered more and more comical excuses to explain why her garden was not at its best. The popularity of the piece meant that any 'resting' garden, which was a riot of colour last month and will be again next month, came to be known as a 'Ruth Draper Garden'.

S

Sadie Hawkin's Dances

Until very recently in Britain there were very few opportunities for a woman to ask a man for a dance or for a date. In America life was not quite so staid. During the 1940s, some high schools ran 'Sadie Hawkin's Dances', at which young ladies could reverse convention and ask a boy to dance. The name comes from Al Capp's, *L'il Abner* comic strip, which was an immensely popular and long-lasting satirical portrait of life in a small town. For one of his plots, Capp invented 'Sadie Hawkin's Day', which was an annual event where single women could chase the unmarried men about town and, if they caught one, marry him on the spot.

Sally Lunn Bun

This is the name given to a particular type of teacake that, it is believed, was first made in eighteenth-century Bath by a pastry cook named Sally Lunn. It has also been suggested that the bun takes its name from the French delicacy, *Soleil Lune*, meaning sun and moon cake.

Scavenger's Daughter

This was the name given to an instrument of torture in the Tower of London, commonly used during the reign of Henry VIII. It took its name from Sir Leonard Skevington, who was the Lieutenant of the Tower when it was introduced. The machine worked by compressing the body, pushing a victim's head against his knees.

Scheherazade

To be dubbed a 'Scheherazade' is high praise indeed, for it means you are an inspiring story teller and a clever woman. The name comes from one of the main stories in *Arabian Nights*, which first appeared in Arabic in the mid-ninth century. It tells of King Schahriah, whose first wife was unfaithful and who, to save himself further pain, pledged to take a new bride every day and have her killed the next morning. His actions threatened all the young girls in his realm and in attempt to try to save them Scheherazade persuaded the king to marry her. She managed to escape the 'morning after' fate by telling her husband a series of stories in instalments and always breaking off at an interesting or exciting point at day break. After a thousand and one nights Schahriah capitulated, and named his clever wife 'the liberator' of her sex. While the first English translation of the *Arabian Nights* was published in 1792, the nineteenth-century orientalist, diplomat and traveller, Sir Richard Burton, translated the first unexpurgated edition in sixteen volumes between 1885 and 1888.

Set One's Cap

An expression that has been in common parlance for two hundred years, it is commonly said that a woman keen to seduce a particular man is 'setting her cap' at him. There are those who argue the expression has its roots in fashion, and that it simply refers to a woman putting on her most fetching bonnet or cap in an attempt to look particularly alluring. Others will tell you that the expression comes from an old French nautical term *mettre le cap sur*, which was the order to turn the prow of a ship in a particular direction. The allusion in this respect was that any woman who had 'set her cap' at a gentleman was intent on sailing his way.

Sex Kitten

Colloquially now used to describe any sexually alluring young woman, 'sex kitten' was originally a nickname given to the French actress, Camille Javal, better known as Brigitte Bardot. Although she had already starred in several French sex-comedy films, Bardot gained international acclaim in

1956 when she starred in the film *And God Created Woman,* written and directed by her first husband, Roger Vadim. In more recent years Brigitte Bardot has devoted her energies and time to animal welfare issues but she is still recognised as being one of the greatest sex symbols of the second half of the twentieth century.

She Who Must Be Obeyed

This expression became popular as a way for a man to describe his 'better half' after it was used in the television series of John Mortimer's *Rumpole of the Bailey*. The wily barrister, Horace Rumpole, used the term whenever he referred to his wife. It is thought that Mortimer's inspiration for the phrase comes from H. Rider Haggard's novel, *She*, published in 1887. In the book we are told that the heroine Ayesha 'was obeyed throughout the length and breadth of the land, and to question her command was certain death'.

Sheila's Day

As well as being an Australian slang term for 'woman', sheila also became the generic name for black female servants during the 1970s in South Africa – the name originally coming from the Irish *caille*, meaning a young girl. 'Sheila's Day' in South Africa is Thursday – traditionally the day that maids and nannies are allowed off work. Sheila is also a variation of Cecilia, one of the early martyrs and the patron saint of music.

Shirley Temple

In the 1930s the American child star Shirley Temple represented all that was cute, angelic and captivating about little girls. By the time she was twelve she had made more than thirty films and her signature tune 'On the Good Ship, Lollipop' was known the world over. She sang and tap-danced her way to international acclaim and at the height of her fame more than a million Shirley Temple dolls flew off the shelves. As an adult she continued to act in several television and radio plays but in the 1960s she turned her attention to public service. Known, after her second marriage, as Shirley Temple Black, in 1969 she became the United States Representative to the United Nations. She was later Ambassador to the Republic of Ghana, the first woman White House Chief of Protocol, a foreign affairs officer with the State Department, and Ambassador to Czechoslovakia.

Shocking Pink

One of the most distinctive and 'girlie' colours, shocking pink was created and named by the Italian fashion designer Elsa Schiaparelli in 1937. At the time the colour was described as a 'crude, cruel, shade of rose' but it has survived all its critics and its creator. The colour became so strongly associated with Schiaparelli, that she called her 1954 autobiography, *Shocking Life*.

Shrinking Violet

According to the traditional language of flowers violets symbolize shyness and modesty. So young women who displayed these characteristics were understandably referred to as 'shrinking violets'.

Siren

A little-known nineteenth-century French scientist is credited with bringing the word 'siren' out of mythology and into everyday speech. In 1819 Baron Cagnard de la Tour invented a device for measuring the vibrations of musical notes which, when partially immersed in water, produced a particular sound reminiscent of a woman's voice. Greek mythology tells several tales of sirens or sea-nymphs whose singing lured sailors to their death and, as his machine also 'sang' underwater, the Baron borrowed the name. His ideas were soon being used to produce fog-warning sirens for steamships. In time a 'siren' was any device that produced a loud noise as a means of warning – rather neatly reversing the original concept of the siren in mythology.

Sitting Pretty

Used in the sense of 'being in an advantageous position', 'sitting pretty' has been in popular usage since the early 1920s when it was first used as the title for an American musical comedy. The phrase subsequently served as the title for several films and novels, as well as becoming established as a widely used turn of phrase.

Sloane Ranger

This is an expression, it is said, that was devised in 1975 by Martina Margretts, a sub-editor on *Harpers & Queen* magazine. It was used to describe a certain type of smart, well-bred, upper-class young woman who lived in, or frequented, Sloane Square in London. When Lady Diana Spencer came to public attention in 1981 she was dubbed 'Supersloane' as an extension of the original expression. While the 'Sloane Ranger' is still a recognisable breed, the expression is seldom used these days.

Spend A Penny

In the 1950s this became a common euphemism for going to the lavatory. It alludes to the charge made for the use of women's public toilets (men's urinals were free), which, in the days before decimal coinage, was usually one penny.

Spend, Spend, Spend

This became the catchphrase of a woman who took retail therapy to the extreme in the 1960s. A coalminer's wife, Vivien Nicholson, won more than a hundred and fifty thousand pounds on the Littlewood's football pools. (It is estimated her win would be worth more than a million pounds today.) When asked what she planned to do with it, she replied 'spend, spend, spend'. Mrs Nicholson was as good as her word and spent all of her money in four years.

Spinster

In the Middle Ages, a spinster was simply a woman who span. In time the expression came also to denote her status, as it was the unmarried women and girls who were mainly occupied with spinning while the married women ran the households. By the early eighteenth century the term was also used to convey the idea of 'old maid'.

Spite Curl

It was once fashionable for women to wear a single curl on their foreheads, for much the same reason as beauty spots were once thought to enhance a woman's beauty. The easiest way to create such a curl was simply by coating a strand of hair in spittle, and so the curls became known as 'spit curls'. This changed in the nineteenth century to 'spite curl' due to the popularity of a rhyme written by the American poet Henry Wadsworth Longfellow:

> There was a little girl and she had a little curl
> Right in the middle of her forehead;
> When she was good, she was very, very, good,
> But when she was bad she was horrid.

There have been various suggestions as to why Longfellow wrote the piece. One of them is that he did so for his daughter, Edith, when she refused to have her hair dressed. Another is that he was attempting to teach a child of his acquaintance the correct pronunciation of the word 'forehead'.

Strait-Laced

Someone who is prudish and prefers the moral high ground is described as being 'strait-laced', an expression that relates, originally, to women's corsets. This often detested item of underwear was introduced to England by the Normans in the eleventh century and remained in fashion, in one form or another, until well into the twentieth century. In the 1700s corsets were laced at the back and to gain the desired shape it was necessary to pull the laces extremely tightly. The figurative use of the term came into being as anyone tightly-corseted or 'strait-laced' had little opportunity to be flexible.

Sugar And Spice

. . . and all that's nice, that's what little girls are made of. The line is from a well-known children's nursery rhyme *What Are Little Boys Made Of?* It has been suggested that it was written around 1820 by the poet laureate, Robert Southey, but it does not feature in his ten-volume collection of poems nor is it mentioned in his biography. It is also said that it was one of the verses that Henry Wadsworth Longfellow, the most popular American poet of the nineteenth century, used to recite. There are more, less well-known verses to the rhyme, one of which asks the question, 'What are young women made of?' The answer, as you might expect, is 'Ribbons and laces, and sweet pretty faces'.

Sweet Fanny Adams

Used nowadays to mean 'nothing at all', the origin of the expression 'sweet Fanny Adams' is particularly gruesome. There was a real Fanny Adams, a little girl who was brutally murdered in 1867 and whose mutilated body was found in the river at Alton in Hampshire. At around the same time the Royal Navy introduced tinned mutton onto the menu for their fleet and the sailors, not impressed with the fare, gave it the nickname 'Sweet Fanny Adams'. Over the succeeding decades the term came to be applied to anything that was considered worthless, and eventually evolved into the usage we know today.

Taffeta Phrases

Taffeta is a name that has been applied to various fabrics beloved by women over the centuries, but these days describes a silk or synthetic material that is crisp, lustrous and usually brightly coloured. In the sixteenth century it referred to a light silken fabric and figuratively the word could mean either 'florid, bombastic' or 'dainty, delicate'. It is the latter sense that is relevant to 'Taffeta Phrases', as it was an expression used to describe euphemisms and poetic language. Shakespeare uses the term in *Love's Labour's Lost*, when Berowne swears to his Rosaline that he will foreswear:

> Taffeta phrases, silken terms precise,
> Three pile'd hyperboles, spruce affectation,
> Figures pedantical;

Tawdry

Now used as a term to describe something garish and shoddy, originally 'tawdry' referred to goods, and in particular silk scarves, called St Audrey's laces, that were sold at a fair held in Ely every October. St Audrey, the patron saint of the city, died in the seventh century, allegedly from a tumour in her throat. As she had always been fond of fine necklaces, she attributed her fatal illness to her worldly vanity. Nevertheless, in her honour the merchants at St Audrey's Fair sold the very goods she ascribed as leading to her downfall, which colloquially were known as 'tawdry laces' (tawdry being a contraction of St Audrey). Initially the scarves were of fine quality, as attested to by Spenser, who in 1579 wrote:

> Bind your fillets faste,
> And girde in your waste,
> For more finesse with a tawdrie lace.

In time, however, the quality of the goods sold at the fair declined and 'tawdry laces' were known throughout Britain for their gaudiness and poor quality. By the eighteenth century the term 'tawdry' was being used to describe anything considered to be garish and cheap.

Three O'Clock Shoes

We have all done it. We have all put on a pair of elegant and fashionable shoes in the morning in the hope they will be comfortable all day, only to find that our are hopes are dashed. Any shoes which start the day comfortably but begin to pinch later on are known colloquially as 'three o'clock shoes', a reference to the time when they usually start to give grief.

Tiara

Once to be found in every aristocratic married woman's jewellery box, a tiara was essential wear for certain evening and state functions, and indeed, we tend to think of a tiara as jewelled headdress for a woman. But originally it was a type of high-peaked cap or turban worn by the Persians and other Easterners, which varied in height and shape depending on the status of the wearer. And when one talks of 'The Tiara', the reference is to the Triple Crown worn by the Pope. It was not until the eighteenth century that the word was used to describe what we know as a 'tiara' today.

Tickled Pink

This is a late nineteenth-century expression meaning to be extremely pleased. The figurative use of 'tickle' was not new, and for centuries it had been recognised how delightful it could be when someone or something 'tickled one's fancy'. It is thought that the Americans came up with the idea that when you were amused to the point of blushing with pleasure, you were 'tickled pink', but the expression is so apposite it rapidly caught on this side of the Atlantic as well.

Tie The Knot

The image of the knot as the interweaving of two sets of emotions has been linked with marriage since ancient times. Brides in ancient Greece wore woollen girdles fastened with a knot said to resemble the interlaced snakes on the rod carried by the god Mercury and the imagery probably dates from an even earlier period. 'Tying the knot' remains a widely used euphemism for getting married, an act in which the married couple bind themselves to each other in a solid and lasting way.

Too Much Fuffle

An old Gaelic word, 'fuffle' could be used either as a noun or a verb. As the latter it meant to 'disarrange', and is the origin of the dialect word 'kerfuffle' meaning a 'scrap' or 'to-do'. As a noun it meant an 'abundance of clothing' and any woman who was considered to be wearing too many frills and flounces would be dismissed as having 'too much fuffle' about her.

Trilby

The soft, broad-brimmed felt hat much beloved by British race goers, takes its name from the eponymous heroine of an 1894 George du Maurier novel. In the stage version of the story, the artist's model, Trilby O'Ferrall, wore a distinctive felt hat. The style was rapidly imitated off-stage and the 'trilby' was born. For a short time following the play 'trilbies' also became a slang term for 'feet', as in both the book and the play there are several references to the sensuous nature of the heroine's bare feet.

Trophy Wife

Although the woman it describes has been identifiable throughout history, the term 'trophy wife' to describe her comes from the 1980s. It is used in a derogatory way to describe the young wife of a wealthy, older man. The implication is that while she may benefit from his position and money, he gains greater status for having a young, attractive woman at his side and in his bed.

Trousseau

The word for a bride's collection of new clothes and linen comes from the French word trousse, meaning 'bundle'. The term came into English in the nineteenth century and, historically, it is a relatively modern idea that a bride should start married life with a newly enhanced wardrobe. Even up until the nineteenth century it was not always customary for a bride to buy a new dress for her wedding. Often she and her party would simply wear their best clothes for the occasion. If a new dress or bonnet were bought, it would likely be used for high days and holidays for years to come.

Twiggy

This was the professional name adopted by one of Britain's most successful models of the 1960s, and stemmed from the fact that she was extremely thin and delicate. Her real name is Lesley Hornby and she was born in Neasdon, London in 1946, but it is as 'Twiggy' she is best known and her beautiful face is still instantly recognisable. Curiously 'twig' in the nineteenth century was a slang word for 'style', and to be 'in twig' was to be very fashionable indeed.

Umbrella

Now an essential item used by both men and women, originally an umbrella was very much a feminine article. In the seventeenth century umbrellas were normally used as sunshades and were made of leather or oiled silk. Heavy and cumbersome, it took another hundred years for umbrellas to become more 'user-friendly'. The use of cane or whalebone to make the ribs made the whole contraption lighter and allowed for a more domed shape. The vagaries of the English climate also meant that the umbrella became an accepted 'protector against rain'. At one time, a self-respecting man would not be seen with an umbrella for fear of being thought effeminate. It was not until the early nineteenth century, when it became fashionable for men to wear top hats, that the umbrella became an accepted item for use by both sexes.

Valley Girl

A common term for a particular type of young American teenager, the expression was first used in the early 1980s in California to describe young girls from the San Fernando Valley. A 'valley girl' is from a reasonably affluent family, loves shopping, junk food, make-up and is fluent in 'Valspeak' – a type of slang. In 1982, the rock artist, Frank Zappa, joined forces with his fifteen-year-old daughter, Moon Unit, to produce a hit song called 'Valley Girl' which includes various 'Valspeak' expressions.

Vamp

The word 'vamp' goes back to Middle English when it referred to the part of a stocking which covered the foot and ankle, or the part of a shoe which covered the front of the foot. As both articles could be repaired or patched, it is from that use that we get the word 'revamp'. The 'femme fatale' sort of 'vamp' is another matter entirely, and the term is generally considered to be an abbreviation of the word 'vampire'. It came into vogue during the early years of silent movies, when such a character appeared in countless films.

Venture Girl

In the mid-nineteenth century, many young English men went to India to seek their fortune or as part of the British army. Any single young woman who set sail in their wake with the intention of finding a husband, was known colloquially as a 'venture girl'.

Venus

The Greeks had Aphrodite but the Roman version of the goddess of love and beauty is Venus. She has been the subject of countless paintings and sculptures and has been the epitome of female loveliness through the ages. One of the most famous statues of the goddess is the Venus de Milo, which stands in the Louvre, in Paris. The sculpture dates from about 100 BC and even though Venus is without arms (it is thought they were broken off when she was buried on the Island of Melos centuries ago), she is considered by many to be one of the finest examples of ancient art still in existence.

Venus Turns Out A Whelp

This rather curious expression comes from the world of gambling. The highest roll of a dice, three sixes, was called a *Venus*, the allusion being to divinity and beauty. The lowest roll, three aces, was known as a *canis*, the Latin word for dog. When 'Venus turns out a whelp' it means that high hopes are dashed – expected success turns out to be a failure.

Veronica Lake

The stage name of the American actress, Constance Ockelman (1919–1973), was once descriptive of a particular hairstyle which she made popular in the 1940s. Her trademark was a long 'peekaboo' bob from behind which she would smile seductively. In modern slang, Veronica Lake is rhyming slang for 'steak'.

Vestal Virgins

Used more in the singular these days than the plural, a 'vestal virgin' is a colloquial term for a girl or woman who is innocent, pure and of impeccable behaviour. The term is taken directly from the six Vestal Virgins who guarded the shrine of Vesta, the goddess of the hearth, in the Forum of ancient Rome. The requirement for a girl to qualify as a Vestal Virgin was that she needed to be as pure as the Sacred Flame which the six tended. If she lost her virginity, the punishment was to be buried alive. If she survived her service for thirty years in purity, she was allowed to marry.

Waif Look

This was the name given to a style that became fashionable in the 1990s. It was personified by models such as Kate Moss, who was described as 'Superwaif'. The 'waif look' involves being extremely thin with an air of fragility and a faux-ragged style of clothes and hair.

Wedding Finger

It is common in Britain for women to wear their wedding rings on the third finger of the left hand. The tradition goes back a long way and comes from the old belief that there was a vein, the *vena amoris*, that ran from the wedding finger directly to the heart. It has also been suggested that the third finger, the pronubus, was also a practical choice. Apart from the fact that the majority of people are right-handed, most people find it more diffi-cult to straighten out their third finger independently of their other fingers. The notion is that it made the third finger on the left hand a safer place on which to wear an important piece of jewellery – and important it was. Today a wedding ring is symbolic but from biblical times onwards, a wedding ring, was 'the seal which gave a wife the right to represent her husband in every way.'

Weeping Brides

Although a girl's wedding day is meant to be one of the happiest of her life, an old custom dictated that she should spend much of the time in tears. Should a bride fail to weep profusely it was thought to be an indication of trouble ahead. The notion stemmed from the belief that a witch could shed no more than three tears, and those only from her left eye. The sight of a weeping bride assured her husband, and the assembled company, that she had not previously 'plighted her troth to Satan'.

Wendy House

The name given to a children's playhouse comes from J. M. Barrie's *Peter Pan: or The Boy Who Would Not Grow Up*. One of the characters is Wendy Darling, who, with her brothers is taken to Never Never Land where Wendy takes on the role of mother to the Lost Boys. The little house constructed for her in the play, first performed in 1904, captured the public imagination and soon all such playhouses became known as 'Wendy Houses'. It is said Barrie named the character 'Wendy' as a tribute to the poet W. E. Henley's daughter. Henley used to refer to Barrie as 'Friend', but Henley's young daughter, too young to enunciate clearly, called Barrie 'Fwendy-Wendy'. Margaret Henley died when she was only six years old, but the author used 'Wendy' as the name of one of his most enduring characters in her honour.

Widow's Cruse

A 'cruse' is an early name for an earthenware pot or jar, and a 'widow's cruse', used figuratively, is an abundance or inexhaustible supply of anything. The allusion is to a biblical story, told in II Kings 4. It tells of a widow whose dead husband's creditors are claiming her two sons in return for his outstanding debt. She tells Elisha that all she has to her name is a small 'cruse' of oil but he bids her to collect as many empty vessels as she can gather and to fill each of the vessels with oil from her own pot. Miraculously she fills all the containers and still has plenty to spare. Elisha then advises her, 'Go, sell the oil, and pay thy debt, and live thou and thy children of the rest'.

Widow's Peak

It was customary in the Middle Ages for women whose husbands had died to wear a distinctive peaked headdress as a badge of widowhood. The front of the head-dress was V-shaped, the point of the V sitting in the middle of the forehead. When the fashion faded, the term 'widow's peak' lived on to describe a hairline that resembled the style. In folklore a natural 'widow's peak' was considered particularly attractive but if it was on a woman it was thought she was destined to be widowed at a young age.

Widow's Weeds

'Weed' is simply an Old English word for a garment or item of clothing, and so 'widow's weeds' were the clothes worn by a woman whose husband had died. Traditionally they were black, to reflect the dark state of the soul, and were worn for eighteen months. For the succeeding three months a widow would be expected to be in 'half-mourning' and again her colour choice was restricted. While it was no longer necessary to wear black, grey, white, lavender or a certain shade of violet were the only colours considered suitable.

Witches' Coven

The word 'coven' is a variation of the word 'convent' which comes from the Latin, *conventus*, meaning 'assembly'. Originally it was a term that could be used to describe any gathering, but in the sixteenth century it became the collective noun for witches after an Act of Parliament in 1543 made witchcraft a felony. James I of England, perhaps influenced by Scotland's harsher treatment of witches, encouraged witch-hunts and the Act of

1603 that made the invoking of evil spirits punishable by death. During the seventeenth century hundreds of women were put on trial. The last execution for witchcraft in England was in 1706 when a woman and her eleven-year-old daughter were hanged, ostensibly for causing their neighbours to spit pins, but the last woman to be convicted of the crime was one Jane Wenham of Hereford. The year was 1712 and Jane was accused of flying. However, fortunately for Jane, the judges decided that there was no law against flying, therefore she had no charge to answer. The laws against witchcraft were finally repealed in England in 1736.

Woman Scorned

Arguably one of the most commonly misquoted phrases relating to women, it comes from *The Mourning Bride*, the only tragedy ever written by the playwright, William Congreve (1670–1729). The full quotation is: 'Heav'n has no rage, like love to hatred turn'd, Nor Hell a fury, like a woman scorn'd'.

Women And Children First

Now often used jocularly when there is a crowd of people attempting to go one way or do the same thing, the origin of the expression is serious. It relates to loss of HMS *Birkenhead* in 1852. The ship was taking troops to the Eastern Cape of South Africa but ran aground fifty miles from the Cape of Good Hope. Only three of the eight lifeboats could be used and the twenty women and children on board were given priority. Four hundred and forty-five soldiers and crew lost their lives in the incident, but the tradition of 'women and children first' was born. In the navy, the code is still known as the 'Birkenhead Drill'.

Xanthippe

Any wife who scolds or berates her husband incessantly can be dubbed a 'xanthippe'. It was the name of Socrates' wife, renowned for her bad temper towards her philosopher husband.